SEAN O'CASEY

WORLD DRAMATISTS

SEAN
O'CASEY

DORIS daRIN

WITH HALFTONE ILLUSTRATIONS

FREDERICK UNGAR PUBLISHING CO.

NEW YORK

Copyright © 1976 by Frederick Ungar Publishing Co.,
  Inc.
Printed in the United States of America
Designed by Edith Fowler

Library of Congress Cataloging in Publication Data

daRin, Doris
  Sean O'Casey.

  (World Dramatists series)
  Includes index.
  Bibliography: p.
  1. O'Casey, Sean, 1880–1964—Criticism and interpretation.
PR6029.C33Z62   822'.9'12   75—10107
ISBN 0—8044—2136—6

FOR J. J. K.

CONTENTS

CHRONOLOGY

1880	Sean O'Casey (John Casey) is born in Dublin to Susan and Michael Casey. He is to remain the youngest of the five surviving Casey children.
ca. 1887	Michael Casey dies, leaving the family in poverty.
1894	O'Casey works in the stockroom of a hardware store, the first of various jobs he is to hold as a teenager.
1900–1910	Becomes involved in the activities of the Gaelic League, the St. Lawrence O'Toole Club, and the Irish Republican Brotherhood. Helps organize the Pipers Band.
1901–11	Works as a laborer on G.N.R.I. (the Irish railways).
1907	O'Casey's first published work, an article on the Irish educational system, appears in *The Peasant and Irish Ireland*.
1911	Writes *The Frost in the Flower* (one-act play) for an amateur group.

Where various sources have disagreed on the dates of premiere performances of O'Casey's plays, the date given is that provided by Eileen O'Casey in the appendix of her book *Sean*.

1913   O'Casey joins James Larkin's Irish Transport and General Workers' Union, which is in the midst of a long-term strike-lockout with Dublin's employers.

1914   Becomes secretary of the Irish Citizen Army; draws up its constitution. 17 July 1914: resigns from the Army because of a disagreement with the executive council.

1916   April: the Easter Rebellion takes place; background of *The Plough and the Stars*.

1918   *Songs of the Wren* (poetry), *More Wren Songs* (poetry), *The Story of Thomas Ashe* (pamphlet), and *The Sacrifice of Thomas Ashe* (pamphlet) are published.
November: O'Casey's beloved mother dies.

1919   *The Story of the Irish Citizen Army* (history) is published.

1919–21   Irish nationalists fight English troops in the Anglo-Irish War; background of *The Shadow of a Gunman*.

1919–22   Three short plays are submitted to and rejected by the Abbey Theatre in Dublin.

1922–23   The Irish Civil War is fought over the terms of the treaty that ends the Anglo-Irish War; background of *Juno and the Paycock*.

1923   *The Shadow of a Gunman* (two-act play) and *Kathleen Listens In* (one-act play) are produced at the Abbey Theatre.

1924   *Juno and the Paycock* and *Nannie's Night Out* (one-act play) are produced at the Abbey Theatre.

1925   O'Casey quits all other work to write full time. *The Shadow of a Gunman* and *Juno and the Paycock* are published.

1926   *The Plough and the Stars* is produced at the Abbey Theatre; the play causes riots by Irish nationalists.
O'Casey visits London to receive the Haw-

thornden Prize for *Juno and the Paycock* and settles there.

1927   Marries Eileen Carey Reynolds, a young actress.

1928   *The Silver Tassie* is published. Its rejection for production by the Abbey Theatre precipitates a feud between O'Casey and Yeats and brings about O'Casey's break with the Abbey.

A son, Breon, is born.

1929   *The Silver Tassie* is premiered at the Apollo Theatre, London.

1932   O'Casey refuses an invitation by Yeats and Shaw to be a founding member of the Irish Academy of Letters.

1933   *Within the Gates* is published.

1934   *Windfalls* (essay, poetry, short stories, two short plays) is published. *Within the Gates* is produced at the Royalty Theatre, London.

O'Casey goes to the U.S. for the American premiere of *Within the Gates*.

1936   A second son, Niall, is born.

1937   *The Flying Wasp* (essays) is published.

1939   *I Knock at the Door* (first volume of autobiography) is published.

A daughter, Shivaun, is born. The family moves from London to Totnes, a small town in southwestern England.

1940   *The Star Turns Red* is published and produced at the Unity Theatre, London. *Purple Dust* is published.

1942   *Red Roses for Me* and *Pictures in the Hallway* (second volume of autobiography) are published.

1943   *Red Roses for Me* is produced at the Olympia Theatre, Dublin.

1945   *Drums under the Windows* (third volume of autobiography) is published. *Purple*

Dust is produced in Liverpool, England, by Old Vic Company.

1946   *Oak Leaves and Lavender* is published.

1947   *Oak Leaves and Lavender* is produced at the Lyric Theatre, London.

1949   *Cock-a-doodle Dandy* is published and produced by an amateur group in England. *Inishfallen, Fare Thee Well* (fourth volume of autobiography) is published.

1951   *Hall of Healing, Bedtime Story,* and *Time to Go* (one-act plays) are published.

1952   *Rose and Crown* (fifth volume of autobiography) is published.

1954   *Sunset and Evening Star* (sixth and final volume of autobiography) is published.

1955   *The Bishop's Bonfire* is published and produced at the Gaiety Theatre, Dublin.
        The family moves near Torquay.

1956   *The Green Crow* (essays and short stories) is published.
        O'Casey's son Niall dies.

1958   *The Drums of Father Ned* is submitted to the theater festival of the Dublin Tostal but withdrawn by O'Casey after objection from the Archbishop of Dublin. O'Casey forbids the production of any of his plays in Ireland.

1959   *The Drums of Father Ned* is produced at the Little Theater, Indiana. *Cock-a-doodle Dandy* is produced at the Edinburgh Festival.

1960   *The Drums of Father Ned* is published.

1961   *Behind the Green Curtains, Figuro in the Night,* and *The Moon Shines on Kylenamoe* (one-act plays) are published.

1962   *Feathers from the Green Crow* (stories, essays, songs, and short plays) is published. An O'Casey Festival of three plays is held at the Mermaid Theatre, London.

1963   *Under a Colored Cap* (essays) is published.

1964   18 September: O'Casey dies of a heart attack at Torquay, England.

1967   *Blasts and Benedictions* (articles and short stories) is published.

SEAN O'CASEY: A PROFILE

Sean O'Casey, christened John Casey, was born in 1880, in Dublin, to Protestants Susan and Michael Casey. He was the last of thirteen children; eight died at birth or in early infancy of a respiratory ailment common to many of Dublin's poor. O'Casey's father, Michael, a truly devout man who read voraciously in religion and related subjects, chose to work for the evangelical Irish Church Mission although he might have earned better wages in some Protestant business firm. As a consequence of his choice, the family, like their Catholic neighbors, struggled for life's necessities. Michael Casey died of a spinal injury when his youngest child was about seven. His widow and their five children slipped down even further among the impoverished of Dublin, sharing the disease-ridden environment and degrading work conditions common to about a third of the city's population.

Nowhere in the western world of the late 1800s

For the reader who wishes to know about the historical events that will frequently be alluded to in the following pages, a brief history of Ireland is offered as an epilogue. The reader is advised to consider the advantages of perusing that epilogue before he reads the book.

could there be found the concentration of ills associated with urban life as in the Dublin of O'Casey's
childhood. Friedrich Engels described the poorer dis-
tricts as "among the most hideous and repulsive to be
seen in the world" (quoted by Gearoid o Tuathaigh, in
Ireland before the Famine 1798/1848, 1972). The
death rate was astronomical: forty-four of every thousand persons perished of illnesses often associated with
malnutrition and neglect. Children comprised a high
part of that figure. Dubliners crowded into old, rotting
buildings, once the elegant mansions of eighteenth-
century aristocrats. These incubators of disease and
desperation were now multifamily units with as many
as eight persons living in a single room. Lavatory and
kitchen facilities originally built to accommodate one
family were now shared by several. And they were
constantly in a state of disrepair. The usually absentee
landlords made no improvements for the most part but
were very careful to collect their rents. Over 30,000 of
the 305,000 population of the city were evicted annu-
ally because they could not pay even the slum tenement rent. Often the meager and dilapidated belong-
ings of some unfortunate family were piled up on the
street outside their former home and they had no
place to go for relief.

Working conditions were equally dreadful for those
who were fortunate enough to have any job whatsoever. The average workweek for a man was seventy to
ninety hours, for which he received about fourteen
shillings; women worked even longer hours than men
for between five and ten shillings; children began
working as early as ten years of age for a crust of
bread. In his excellent study on O'Casey, *Sean
O'Casey: The Man and His Work* (1962), David
Krause commented that the "lower class Dubliners
had little to look forward to beyond disease, drunken-
ness, and death."

Susan Casey tried desperately to keep her family alive and healthy despite the filth, ignorance, and despair of tenement life. Without her efforts, O'Casey believed that he himself would not have survived. Sickly at birth, he contracted chronic ulceration of the cornea that caused him terrible pain and was to weaken his sight for life. Any eyesight at all was retained through the heroic efforts of his mother, who took him to a clinic miles from their home for treatment.

Because of his poor eyesight, O'Casey was forced to end his formal schooling after only a few months in the Protestant school. But his mother constantly encouraged a natural curiosity in the child for knowledge. When O'Casey was fourteen, he made his first serious effort to teach himself to read and write, working from old primers and a dictionary from his father's library. The book he used most frequently—so important a part of his Protestant training—was the Bible, which served as a book of wonder and adventure.

When O'Casey was about twelve, he came into contact with the world of the theater. One of his older brothers was active in an amateur theatrical troupe that performed scenes from Shakespeare and Dion Boucicault, the nineteenth-century melodramatist. In those days, many Dubliners preferred Boucicault to Shakespeare and young O'Casey shared their sentiments. As he later recalled it, his opinion of the time was "Shakespeare's good in bits, but, for colour and stir, give me Boucicault." But he was soon using the bard's plays to learn to read as he had earlier used the Bible: "I learnt to read by Shakespeare and used to act scenes from the plays in my room. When I was 17, I could recite whole passages from Hamlet, MacBeth [sic], and Julius Caesar by heart" (quoted by T. C. Cunliffe, in the periodical *Time & Tide*, XVI).

In his early adolescence, O'Casey began working in

various Protestant firms—crockery, stationer, newspaper distributór—at menial, backbreaking tasks, and
he was considered fortunate to be able to earn a few
shillings a week. But he resigned from one job after
another because he could not show his employers the
deference they expected. On one occasion he refused
to take off his cap when receiving his weekly pittance
and was fired then and there.

But young O'Casey's spirit was not based on arrogance or vanity; it was based on the fact that he realized his employers were meager, shallow men who, as
he described many of them later in life, gave up learning as soon as they left school. But O'Casey himself
was learning because he loved it. Thanks to his father's
library and a few pennies he had been able to save
from his wages, O'Casey had read, in addition to the
Globe edition of Shakespeare and translations of the
classics, books by Dickens, Scott, Balzac, Hugo, Rus-
kin, Darwin, Fenimore Cooper, Dumas, Tacitus,
Reade, Carlyle, Mignet, Bunyan, Sheridan, Goldsmith,
Byron, Shelley, Keats, Crabbe, Tennyson, Gray—an
incredible achievement for a poor boy with failing
eyesight. These books were the source of O'Casey's
pride in himself and his refusal to do obeisance to any
man on the grounds of money: "For the moment
Johnny existed only for himself, and in himself. They
were foolishness; he was wisdom. He had the whip
hand over them, for he knew more than they did, now.
His mind was a light that lighteth every man that
cometh into the world" (*Pictures in the Hallway*,
1942).

During his middle to late twenties, O'Casey became
a laborer on the Great Northern Railroad, where he
first wielded pick and shovel and then became a brick-
layer. During these years, O'Casey became increasingly aware of his own "Irishness." As a Protestant
child in a predominantly Catholic environment, he

was alienated from many of his playmates who had learned from their parents to hate the English tyrants —his family was loyal to the English government and saw it as protecting them. When O'Casey was very young, a playmate had told him only Catholics were really Irish. But when he repeated the remark to his mother, she angrily reassured him that he was indeed Irish too.

As O'Casey read the history of his country, he discovered that a large number of Ireland's champions were Protestants. O'Casey immersed himself in Irish history, language, and culture. He attended Gaelic League classes, in which he learned to speak and write Irish. Whatever spare time remained was devoted to trying to convince his fellow Irishmen—Catholics as well as Protestants—of the importance of learning Irish culture. O'Casey even tried to have portions of the Protestant Book of Common Prayer published in Irish.

At the same time, O'Casey was drawn toward the political struggle of the nationalists. Although raised in a home loyal to the English government, he came to know Ireland's history of oppression and economic exploitation. He became friendly with a Catholic tram conductor who helped win him over to Fenianism, and sometime in his early manhood, he joined the Irish Republican Brotherhood, the small but dedicated Fenian organization that remained faithful to the goal of complete Irish independence. O'Casey wrote fundraising pleas and tried to recruit members for the Brotherhood.

In about 1907, O'Casey joined the St. Lawrence O'Toole Club. Although some of its members were militant nationalists, the club was primarily a social group that gathered for Irish songs and dances. O'Casey and Frank Cahill, another member, became close friends and together organized a group of bagpipe players called the St. Lawrence O'Toole Pipers Band, which is still active today.

In 1911, O'Casey was dismissed by the Great Northern Railroad, ostensibly for "habitual neglect of work." Actually, for some time he had been defying the management by refusing, among other rebellious acts, to join a company-sponsored pension plan. And he was openly sympathetic to James Larkin's independent Irish Transport and General Workers' Union, considered an anathema to his employers. After being discharged, O'Casey was unemployed for a long period of time, he and his mother often near starvation. Gaunt, with red-rimmed and watery eyes, he usually wore the shabby clothes of the workman—cap, muffler, jacket, and hobnailed boots. But he continued to participate in several Irish cultural, political, and social organizations.

These terrible years of poverty undoubtedly contributed to O'Casey's development as a communist. He lived in the midst of squalid slums where families existed on the verge of starvation. He saw his three brothers physically and spiritually deteriorate as they turned to drink to alleviate the frustrations of their life. He saw his married sister's family descend from one form of degradation to another because money was lacking for even minimal medical care. O'Casey came to despise those forces he felt joined together in victimizing the common man: the government and its politicians, the self-satisfied middle class, the clergy itself.

Although O'Casey had been confirmed in the Irish Protestant Church and deeply respected some of the pastors of his parish, he was more and more alienated from every form of institutionalized religion. He embraced the revolutionary principles from which the Christian church had evolved, fervently believing in the reorganization of society on the basis of the brotherhood of man in a state of equality, justice, and love. But he felt that the church had sacrificed these ideals to political and economic expedience. It taught passivity instead of revolution; it fostered the twin crimes of poverty and wealth; it wasted young lives by insisting on a "ferocious" puritanism; and it preached superstitious dogma.

O'Casey always remained greatly influenced by his extensive knowledge of the Bible, but he rejected orthodox Christianity and became increasingly anticlerical. His extensive reading of Darwin and G. B. Shaw led him far away from what he came to call the "magicjestic" story of man's fall in the Bible, once believed by O'Casey to have been handed down from heaven, straight from the hand of God.

Just as O'Casey became disillusioned with the church, so he became disillusioned with the Gaelic League and the Irish Republican Brotherhood because of what he felt were their narrowly defined goals, which had little or nothing to do with the needs of the working class. Alluding to the prophet Ezekiel (chapter 37), O'Casey described Ireland as covered with dry bones. In a particularly moving passage in *Drums under the Windows* (1945), the third volume of his autobiography, he asked: "Who would be the first to make an army out of these active and diligent dry bones? Who the first to breathe into them a breath from the flame of endeavour and strife and defiance? Whose lips would first be touched by a red coal from God's altar?"

His answer was James Larkin, the impassioned orator and uncrowned king of Dublin's working class. O'Casey saw Larkin as an Irish Prometheus who had come to Dublin to save its impoverished inhabitants from capitalist exploitation, religious meekness, and self-despair. "Throughout the streets he strode," O'Casey later recalled, "shouting into every dark and evil-smelling hallway. 'The great day of change has come: Circe's swine had a better time than you have; come from your vomit; out into the sun. Larkin is calling you all.'" O'Casey joined Larkin's Irish Transport and General Workers' Union shortly after the beginning of the 1913 strike-lockout and became a close friend of his. (It was Larkin who introduced O'Casey to the dramatic writings of Eugene O'Neill.)

O'Casey also became secretary of the Irish Citizen Army, the union's paramilitary arm organized during the strike-lockout; its banner was called the Plough and the Stars—the title O'Casey was later to give to one of his most memorable plays. In a reorganization of the Army, O'Casey drafted its constitution and worked feverishly for recruits.

After Larkin sailed to America in 1914, James Connolly, the zealous socialist and nationalist, became the union leader. When Connolly fostered an alliance between the Irish Citizen Army and the prestigious Irish Volunteers—a paramilitary group devoted to the cause of Irish freedom and including among its ranks many politicians and middle-class employers—O'Casey condemned the alliance as a betrayal of working-class ideals. And he was saddened to note that many members of the Irish Citizen Army were drawn to the more respectable Irish Volunteers. In a confrontation with the Army's executive council on the issue of dual membership in both organizations, O'Casey was voted down. He resigned from the Army in July 1914.

While involved in the Gaelic League, the General Transport and Workers' Union, and the Irish Republican Brotherhood (from which he had by now also resigned), O'Casey had written many cultural, political, and educational articles that appeared in various newspapers and journals. He was something of a public figure in Dublin because of these activities. After quitting the Irish Citizen Army, however, he devoted his considerable energies more specifically to the world of books and the arts. He continued his membership in the St. Lawrence O'Toole Club, where he spent long hours discussing his favorite authors. Twice a week he participated in the *ceilidh* nights, when club members sang traditional ballads, as well as songs that he had written, and danced to Irish folk music.

Those who knew O'Casey in this period of his life— when he was in his middle and late thirties—held varying opinions of him. To some, he was gruff, humorless, aloof, reticent, full of pride; others spoke of his marvelous sense of humor and booming laugh, of his patience with the problems of the younger club members who sought his advice, and of his utter lack of hostility or self-pity in the face of overwhelming odds. But on one point virtually everyone was agreed: O'Casey was a brilliant man who had read widely and was gifted with a talent for words.

O'Casey's resignation from the Irish Citizen Army excluded him from organized resistance to English rule; thus he did not participate in the Easter Rebellion that took place in April 1916. But because he was known in Dublin as a nationalist, he was arrested by English soldiers and interned along with the militant nationalists. Shortly after the rebellion was quashed, however, he was released from the granary where he had been imprisoned.

Of the Easter Rebellion, O'Casey wrote that it was "the Year One in Irish history and Irish life began." He noted the shift of public opinion as Dublin's citizens, once indifferent to the national cause, watched the public execution of the rebels with growing disgust and hatred toward the English. "Cathleen, daughter of Houlihan, walks firm now, a flush on her haughty cheek. She hears the murmur in the people's hearts.

Her lovers are gathering around her, for things are changed, changed utterly" (*Drums under the Windows*).

But, although O'Casey spoke of the martyrs of the rebellion as the "poor dear dead men" and respected some for their valor, he felt that many had victimized themselves and innocent bystanders in a romantic ecstasy of playing soldiers: vanity, so much was vanity.

More importantly, O'Casey felt that the Easter Rebellion did not have the support of the working class because its leaders were indifferent to the needs of this class. He understood, as the rebels could not, how it was possible for this poor, starving populace to plunder and loot in Dublin's chaotic streets while Ireland's heroes marched to suicide. O'Casey felt that even James Connolly, the socialist leader of the union and one of the leaders in the rebellion, failed to comprehend the workers' hope for a better, happier life.

Despite his continued anti-English sentiments, O'Casey also remained only a spectator throughout the bloody Anglo-Irish War (1919–21). He refused to believe that killing English soldiers could really help the cause of Irish freedom, and he was concerned for the people who died in the crossfire of the antagonists. O'Casey even began to drift away from the St. Lawrence O'Toole Club, whose new members were more interested in professional terrorism than in Irish culture; and his friendship with Cahill had already begun to deteriorate over political and religious issues. Finally, O'Casey quit the club and the Pipers Band.

In 1920, O'Casey moved into a slum tenement with Michael Mullin, an old union friend. His beloved mother had died in 1918; his sister and his favorite brother were also dead; and another brother had left Ireland for England. Now O'Casey severed ties with the one remaining member of his family, his brother

Michael, whose heavy drinking and belligerence had always caused the two to argue bitterly.

O'Casey was particularly incensed with his brother because he made it impossible for him to read or to write. Under very difficult circumstances, he had published two volumes of verse, *Songs of the Wren* (1918) and *More Wren Songs* (1918), and three other books, *The Story of Thomas Ashe* (1918), *The Sacrifice of Thomas Ashe* (1918), and *The Story of the Irish Citizen Army* (1919). Between 1919 and 1922, he also tried his hand at writing drama, which had interested him since his childhood days. He submitted "The Frost in the Flower," "The Harvest Festival," and "The Crimson in the Tri-Colour" to the prestigious Abbey Theatre for production—all were rejected as promising but inadequate. Nevertheless he was determined that one day the Abbey would produce one of his plays.

Unfortunately the manuscripts of these early ventures were lost through the carelessness of those asked to read them. The terrible conditions under which O'Casey worked made their loss even more bitter. Since he had no money for paper and ink, he had to rely on friends who worked in offices to make off with batches of paper and boxes of indelible lead pencils. By boiling the purple lead in water, O'Casey could then concoct a pot of homemade ink.

When the Irish Civil War (1922–23) began, O'Casey condemned both sides: he felt that the new Free State government was indifferent to the needs of the working class; and the Republican movement had been taken over by members of the middle class seeking a way to fatten their purses. Although he became increasingly repulsed by the brutal torture and murder of the war, he nevertheless aligned himself with the Republican movement as the lesser of two evils and, for a time, wrote publicity and propaganda to further its aims.

In 1923 the Abbey Theatre finally accepted a two-act play by O'Casey for production: *The Shadow of a Gunman*, which became a tremendous popular success. Later that same year, the Abbey produced his one-act play *Kathleen Listens In*; this was followed in 1924 by the very successful full-length *Juno and the Paycock*, and another one-acter, *Nannie's Night Out*.

O'Casey's association with the Abbey Theatre was mutually advantageous. By 1923 the Abbey was in a precarious financial position, and O'Casey's plays saved it from bankruptcy. They were informed by a social and political awareness of the contemporary scene hitherto lacking in the theater's repertory, hence their popular appeal. O'Casey developed a particularly gratifying friendship with Lady Augusta Gregory, a director of the theater who had encouraged him to continue writing.

Then, in February 1926, the Abbey Theatre produced O'Casey's new play, *The Plough and the Stars*; his popularity quickly plummeted downward. The play portrayed the rebels of the Easter Rebellion in an antiheroic and unsentimental light. It juxtaposed in a way the public could not accept, the conversation of tipsy characters in a bar and the speeches of the martyred Padraic Pearse being delivered outside the bar. Irate patriots denounced O'Casey as vulgar and as a traitor to the Irish nation. Members of Dublin's literary circles also joined in the attack. Incensed by these accusations, O'Casey wrote in his autobiographical *Inishfallen, Fare Thee Well* (1949):

> For the first time in his life, Sean felt a surge of hatred for Cathleen ní Houlihan sweeping over him. He saw now that the one who had the walk of a queen could be a bitch at times. She galled

the hearts of her children who dared to be above
the ordinary, and she often slew her best ones. . . .
What an old snarly gob she could be at times; an
ignorant one too.

At the end of February 1926, O'Casey packed his
few personal effects and his books and set sail for
England. Intending the journey as a brief vacation
from Ireland, he was, instead, to live in England for
the rest of his life.

Six weeks after O'Casey's arrival, he was awarded
the coveted Hawthornden Prize for *Juno and the Paycock*, then playing successfully in London. The
"dreamy-eyed, shabbily dressed man who a year ago
was a builder's laborer," as the *New York Times* described him, was suddenly lionized by English aristocrats and celebrities. Many of his new admirers unconsciously patronized O'Casey as a noble Irish proletarian who had sprung out of some mythic peat bog
fully equipped for the writing of drama. Given
O'Casey's arduous study habits, his endless reading
and writing, this romantic view of his artistry and craft
could not have been further from the truth. O'Casey
considered himself a disciplined artist, with an education far superior to many who had had the benefit of
formal university training.

Soon after arriving in London, O'Casey met Eileen
Carey Reynolds, a beautiful, young, Irish-born actress.
Miss Reynolds had been touring in New York in a
musical comedy when she first read O'Casey's *Juno
and the Paycock*. Profoundly moved by the tragedy,
she determined that one day not only would she play
the role of Mary Boyle, but she would meet the playwright as well. Shortly after her return to London,
Miss Reynolds and O'Casey were introduced by a
friend of hers. When she was asked to play the role of

Nora Clitheroe in *The Plough and the Stars*, soon to open in London, O'Casey personally directed her in rehearsals and encouraged her during the three weeks she played the role.

Their relationship continued and, despite bitter objections from her mother, they were married on 23 September 1927. After a brief visit to Ireland, the newlyweds settled in London. O'Casey was then nearing completion of a new play entitled *The Silver Tassie*, an expressionistic antiwar play, which in style and theme was a departure from his earlier works. The Abbey Theatre directors expressed the hope that he would let them produce it. At the insistence of Lennox Robinson, an Abbey director, O'Casey sent a completed copy of the play off to Dublin the moment it was available.

In April 1928, however, on the day of the birth of his first son, Breon, O'Casey received a letter from Yeats rejecting *The Silver Tassie* in a very uncomplimentary and patronizing tone. Stunned by the rejection and profoundly hurt by Yeats, O'Casey wrote a scathing letter in return, denouncing Yeats for permitting his personal bias in drama to overcome his sense of objectivity about innovation in the theater. The bitter exchange between the two men virtually ended O'Casey's close relationship with the Abbey Theatre. The furor eventually died down, and years later O'Casey became friendly once again with Yeats. But everyone was diminished by the rupture and the Abbey never again nurtured as fine a dramatist as O'Casey.

In the years following, O'Casey continued to write plays in an experimental mode and found that most English producers, with the exception of C. B. Cochran, were reluctant to undertake any production that did not promise commercial success. Thus O'Casey often found himself deeply in debt. In 1934, hopeful that a New York success would bring much-needed money, he accepted an invitation to visit the United States to help publicize the production there of his new play, *Within the Gates*. He arrived in New York to the same kind of popular acclaim accorded him in London in 1926. For the first time, he met Eugene O'Neill and George Jean Nathan, both of whom became lifelong friends. Although reasonably successful in New York, *Within the Gates* encountered censorship problems on a subsequent tour, which soon halted the tour altogether.

In 1936 a second son, Niall, was born to the O'Caseys and then a daughter, Shivaun, in 1939, the same year the family moved from London to Totnes, a small town in southwestern England. Their primary reason for the move was to find a good, inexpensive school system for the children and a cheaper rent than what they had been paying. For approximately the next fifteen years, O'Casey devoted much of his time to the writing of his autobiography, which fills six long volumes, as well as plays, which were frequently published before they ever saw the boards.

In 1955 the family moved again, to a town near Torquay. O'Casey continued writing plays and articles. Although his articles usually dealt with literary subjects, he frequently voiced in them his views on political and economic questions. O'Casey often wielded a "two-edged sword of thought," which caused conflicts with directors, critics, editors, and fellow writers. Undoubtedly, these confrontations with some of the most powerful men in the literary world were not helpful to the financial success of O'Casey's career. In the course of time, he came to look to the United States for sympathy with his work and for a livelihood.

Notwithstanding the problems he encountered, O'Casey maintained his philosophy of vitalism and his phenomenal capacity for work. By his seventies, he was frail in health and almost blind, an insufferable condition for a man who so loved to read, but his creative output continued. The most terrible blow of all was to come, however. In 1956 his son Niall died of leukemia at the age of twenty. O'Casey was nearly broken by the tragedy. In an essay entitled "Under a Greenwood Tree He Died," the bereft father wrote:

> My bitterest pain of remembrance is not of our loss, not of mine, but of his. . . . My boy, my heart-loved boy, death came to you like a damned thief in the daytime, when all was young and everything was bright and brave and life was dancing.

In 1955 *The Bishop's Bonfire*, a play satirizing clericalism in Ireland, had premiered at the Gaiety Theatre in Dublin. And in 1957, when O'Casey was asked to submit a play for Dublin's Tostal, an annual spring festival of plays and music, he sent the light-hearted comedy *The Drums of Father Ned*. Not nearly as critical of the clergy as was *The Bishop's Bonfire*, Dublin's Archbishop nevertheless refused to sanction the Tostal if O'Casey's play and a dramatized version of Joyce's *Ulysses* were performed. The irate O'Casey withdrew his play and refused to permit any future performances of his works in Ireland.

In the last few years of O'Casey's life, there was a reawakening of interest in his plays, both in the United States and in Europe. He was particularly pleased with the success of his favorite play, *Cock-a-doodle Dandy*, at the 1959 Edinburgh Festival. When the production was taken to London, he went to a performance; it was the first time in many years that he had entered the theater.

Sean O'Casey died on 18 September 1964, at the age of eighty-four, his hand clasping that of his beloved wife, "the pulse of my heart," as he lovingly described her.

In his total commitment to the task of writing effective drama, O'Casey addressed himself to every aspect. In meticulous stage directions, he established every detail that would appear on stage during the course of the drama, such as stage properties and their exact placement on stage. Indeed, in those productions of his plays that ignore these details or replace them with others, significant dimensions are invariably lost. Because this detail is integral to each play, a good deal of it is offered in the following pages.

THE MAJOR PLAYS

The Shadow of a Gunman

The Shadow of a Gunman: A Tragedy in Two Acts was produced in 1923 at the Abbey Theatre in Dublin. The play takes place during the violent period of the so-called Anglo-Irish War, when the Irish Republican Army was engaged in guerrilla warfare with the English Black and Tans. One of the tactics used by the Irish was to strike the enemy and run; they were often hidden by sympathetic citizens, who referred to them as "gunmen on the run."

O'Casey specified the time of the play as May 1920, which would have been shortly after the English authorities had imposed an early curfew on Dublin in the hope of curbing the gunmen. Despite the curfew, raids, ambushes, killings, reprisals, and arrests continued to escalate: Dublin became an armed camp with innocent bystanders often killed in the crossfire.

The plot of *The Shadow of a Gunman* revolves around two cowardly Irishmen who permit an idealistic, romantic young girl to be arrested by English soldiers on the charge of possessing bombs when responsibility for the bombs is theirs. Subsequently, she dies in an ambush on the way to prison. The drama is set in Hilljoy Square, a tenement slum in Dublin. Both acts of the play take place in what was known as a "return room," that is, a back parlor facing a yard. Two large windows occupy most of the back wall.

The first act takes place in midday. The curtain rises on the two occupants of the return room: the peddler Seumas Shields, middle-aged, unkempt and slovenly in appearance, is lying on one of the two beds in the room; the poet Donal Davoren, in his early thirties, rather good-looking and neatly dressed, is typing at a table. The room itself is untidy; scattered about are books, ties, collars, and cooking utensils. On the mantelshelf, a statue of the Virgin Mary is to the right, a crucifix in the center, and a Sacred Heart to the left. These religious objects belong to Seumas. The candlestick, wild flowers, books, and writing materials on the table are Davoren's.

As Davoren types, he hums a song he is composing. The voices of two women (one at the door, the other at the windows) begin to shout for Seumas to wake up and get out of bed. Their repeated cries to the sleeping man create a jarring contrast to Davoren's gentle humming. When Seumas finally awakens and sends the women away, he grumbles that his fellow peddler Maguire had promised to pick him up earlier in the day to begin work.

As Seumas clambers slowly out of bed, he and Davoren begin to argue about the nature of philosophy, religion, and literature. Davoren tries to stop the conversation and continue writing, but Seumas speaks on without hesitation. Finally, Davoren stops writing and sighs, "Ah me! alas, pain, pain, ever, for ever!" (This quotation, which he repeats several times throughout the play, is from Shelley's *Prometheus Unbound.*)

The two men continue to argue until Maguire rushes into the room with the announcement that he cannot work that day but must go to Knocksedan, a district on the outskirts of Dublin. Despite Seumas's protests, Maguire places a small bag, presumably containing household wares, in a corner and hurries out. As he exits, Mulligan, the owner of the tenement, arrives and insists upon speaking to Seumas. He is very angry with him for not paying the rent and for writing letters of complaint about the condition of the tenement to the newspapers. He is also annoyed with Seumas for lodging Davoren in the room without permission. Threatening them with legal action, Mulligan blusters out.

According to Seumas, Mulligan and most of the other tenants in the building believe that Davoren is a "gunman on the run," and he wants him out of the house before trouble starts. Davoren is surprised. After Seumas leaves for work, Davoren goes back to his typing and is interrupted almost immediately by a knocking on the door. He refuses to answer, but Minnie Powell, a very pretty young neighbor, walks in and asks to borrow some milk. At first Davoren is irritated by her, but Minnie's talk about a desire for a better life, her independence, and her spirit arouse his interest. Like Mulligan, Minnie believes Davoren to be a "gunman on the run," a mistake he encourages because the image appeals to his vanity. Minnie is obviously infatuated with Davoren.

While they are talking, Tommy Owens—a small, thin man with a nasal drawl caused by constant drinking and smoking—comes to visit "the gunman." After stammering his admiration for Davoren, he suddenly breaks out into song, "God Save Ireland," and reduces himself to tears. In the midst of his performance, Mr. Gallogher and Mrs. Henderson, also tenement neighbors, come into the room looking for Davoren. They have come to ask his help in a matter concerning a lawsuit.

Mr. Gallogher, a spare little man with a nervous

voice and hesitant manner, brings a letter he has written to the courts established by the Dáil Éireann, the outlawed rebel government. His neighbors, the Dwyers, are threatening him with violence, and he asks Davoren to expedite his petition by delivering the letter personally. He reads aloud with great self-importance:

> The name of the resident-tenant who is giving all this trouble and who, pursuant to the facts of the case aforesaid, mentioned, will be the defendant, is Dwyer. The husband of the aforesaid Mrs. Dwyer, or the aforesaid defendant, as the case may be, is a seaman, who is coming home shortly, and we beg The Irish Republican Army to note that the said Mrs. Dwyer says he will settle us when he comes home. While leaving it entirely in the hands of the gentlemen of The Republican Army, the defendant, that is to say, James Gallogher of fifty-five St. Teresa Street, ventures to say that he thinks he has made out a Primmy Fashy [prima facie] Case against Mrs. Dwyer and all her heirs, male and female as aforesaid mentioned in the above written schedule.

During the interview, Mrs. Henderson, a good-natured massive woman, behaves with deferential self-assurance toward Davoren. She, like the others, has the notion that Davoren is hiding out with Seumas because of his rebel activities.

A newsboy outside the windows shouts that a gunman named Maguire has been killed in an English ambush at Knocksedan. Davoren recognizes the name of Seumas's partner but denies knowing Maguire to his visitors.

Everyone leaves except Minnie, who is concerned about Davoren's safety. She asks him to type her name and his on a piece of paper as a love memento. Amused but flattered by the request, Davoren complies and gives her the typewritten paper. They embrace one another, and Minnie leaves.

By this point Davoren himself is quite attracted to the girl. "Very pretty, but very ignorant," he muses aloud; and he wonders what danger could exist to himself in being the *shadow* of a gunman to gratify the deluded Minnie's notion that he is a real one.

Act II of the play opens on the evening of the same day, after curfew. Again Davoren is typing at the table and Seumas is lounging in bed. The bag left earlier by Maguire is still in the corner of the room. The two men begin to argue about the nature of true poetry. Seumas contends that a poet is great only insofar as he can inspire the common people with his words; Davoren counters that the common people are without regard for poetic beauty, hence unimportant to the poet. Interrupting Davoren, Seumas says he can hear a mysterious tapping in the wall; he believes it can bode no good for the future.

Unable to work because of Seumas's constant chatter, Davoren angrily gets into bed. Their conversation turns to the war that is raging in the streets. The whole country, Seumas complains, has gone mad with fighting, the Irish as well as the English. Davoren remembers a time when Seumas himself "believed in nothing but the gun." Seumas retorts:

> Ay, when there wasn't a gun in the country; I've a different opinion now when there's nothin' but guns in the country. . . . An' you daren't open your mouth, for Kathleen ni Houlihan is very different now to the woman who used to play the harp an' sing. . . . for she's a ragin' divil now, an' if you only look crooked at her you're sure of a punch in th' eye.

Seumas continues that the Irish will not defeat the English army by killing an occasional English soldier, and very often innocent civilians are killed by the combatants.

In the course of the conversation both men insist that their pacifist attitudes have nothing to do with a fear of death. Seumas finds there is a great comfort in religion that makes "a man strong in time of trouble an' brave in time of danger." Davoren finds his comfort in philosophy: "philosophy that makes the coward brave; the sufferer defiant; the weak strong; the . . ." While he is speaking, a volley of shots is heard in a lane that runs parallel to the wall of the backyard. Both men dive under the covers, "religion and philosophy . . . forgotten in the violent fear of a nervous equality," as O'Casey comments in his stage directions.

The Black and Tans and the Irish gunmen are sniping at each other in the darkened streets. Seumas is worried about a stable in the back of their tenement, reputed by the neighbors to be a rebel bomb factory. Davoren is furious that Seumas never mentioned its existence to him before.

A mousy woman with a cowed, abject air enters the room. Mrs. Grigson, their downstairs neighbor, is concerned about her husband, who is still out despite the curfew. He has no life insurance, she tells them. Grigson himself stumbles drunkenly into the room and in a boisterous voice tries to engage the two men in conversation. He insists with pride that he is an Orangeman (that is, an Irish Protestant), who considers the Bible the absolute and final word of God. "I know how to keep Mrs. Grigson in her place," he says. "I have the authority of the Bible for that . . . Holy Scripture . . . says, 'The woman shall be subject to her husband.' "

Meanwhile, the sound of a truck comes closer and closer until it stops near the tenement. Mrs. Grigson fears that the English soldiers are coming to arrest

Davoren, who was described as a gunman by Tommy
Owens in a bar that evening. Shooting begins again,
and the Grigsons flee to their basement apartment.
Frantic with fear, Davoren searches for the letter addressed to the courts of the rebel government,
given him earlier in the day by Gallogher. He finds the
letter and burns it. Seumas insists that he look into
Maguire's bag, and Davoren discovers that it contains
homemade bombs, not household wares as he had
supposed.

Minnie rushes into the room to tell them that the
Black and Tans have surrounded the tenement. When
the hysterical men tell her about the bombs, Minnie
offers to take the bag to her room. If the soldiers find
them, they may not be as hard on a girl as they would
be on a man. Minnie runs out of the room, carrying
the bag as the two men cower in terror on their beds.

The Black and Tans are heard breaking into the
house, and one enters the room to search for contra-
band ammunition. Mrs. Grigson comes in with the
news that some of them are making Grigson sing
Catholic hymns, despite his insistence that he is a
Protestant and loyal to the English government. They
are also drinking his whiskey. The soldier hurries out
to join his comrades.

Loud, angry voices are heard in the hallway above.
Some of the soldiers have found the bag of bombs in
Minnie's room and are shoving her down the stairs and
outside into the waiting truck. She can be heard shouting bravely, if a little hysterically, "Up the Republic,"
the battlecry of the Irish Republican Army. Mrs. Henderson, who had tried to defend Minnie from the soldiers, is also being shoved along by them into the
truck.

Seumas is desperately afraid that Minnie may tell
the soldiers the truth about the bombs' ownership;
Davoren is afraid that she may be harmed by them,

but he never moves from his bed to help her. When it quiets down outside, the Grigsons appear at the door. She commiserates with her husband over what he suffered at the hands of the English soldiers. Embarrassed that Davoren and Seumas should know of his cowardice, Grigson orders her back to their apartment.

All three men begin to brag about their aggressive behavior with the soldiers during the raid, but with the sound of loud explosions from outside, they run wildly for cover. A few minutes pass, and Mrs. Grigson reappears with a solemn air. Irish gunmen ambushed the truck as it was pulling away from the tenement with the prisoners. Minnie, who tried to jump off during the fray, was shot through the bosom by her own people. A bloodied scrap of paper bearing her name was found on the dead girl's breast. It is the typewritten paper on which Davoren had typed their names; his has been obliterated by the blood.

Davoren moans, "Ah me, alas! Pain, pain, pain ever, for ever! . . . Oh, Davoren, Donal Davoren, poet and poltroon, poltroon and poet!" Seumas's comment on the incident is that he knew something "bad" would come of the mysterious tapping he heard in the wall earlier.

The story of *The Shadow of a Gunman* had its origin in an actual incident that occurred during the Anglo-Irish War when O'Casey was sharing a tenement room with Michael Mullin, an old union friend. One night the tenement was raided by the Black and Tans, who were looking for a concealed bomb factory. For hours, the inhabitants were terrorized by the soldiers. It turned out that O'Casey's seemingly timid, supposedly apolitical landlord was actually a gunman for the Irish Republican Army.

O'Casey started to work on *The Shadow of a Gunman* two years after the incident described above. In October 1922, he wrote a letter about the play to Lennox Robinson, a director at the Abbey Theatre. Robinson quoted the letter in his autobiographical *Curtain Up* (1942):

> I am engaged on a play at present—*On the Run*—the first act is finished and most of the second. It deals with the difficulties of a poet who is in continual conflict with the disturbances of a tenement house, and is built on the frame of Shelley's phrase: "Ah, me, alas, pain, pain, ever, forever."

Submitted to the Abbey about a month later, the play was accepted for immediate production. No revisions were considered necessary except for a title change because there was already an Abbey play entitled *On the Run*.

In the play, O'Casey portrayed male characters who suffer from a moral paralysis and cowardice at variance with their heroic words; the women characters say little about their personal bravery, but they perform acts of heroism and even self-sacrifice. Donal Davoren is the antihero who describes himself in the final scene as "poet and poltroon." Some of the difficulties facing Davoren are based on those O'Casey himself suffered when he wrote his plays in the overcrowded tenement room shared with Michael Mullin. Although O'Casey might have sympathized with the frustrations of such a character, Davoren alienates our sympathy by the inner conflict mirrored in his face as well as in his speech and behavior. In the stage directions, O'Casey mockingly described the face of Davoren as "an eternal war between weakness and strength." Davoren quotes lines spoken by Shelley's tragic hero Prometheus, as if they applied to himself. But his cowardice when Minnie is arrested turns the lines into unconscious self-mockery.

Seumas Shields, the roommate of Davoren, was based on O'Casey's friend Michael Mullin. Like Mullin, Seumas typifies many Irishmen who became deeply involved in nationalist organizations, both of a cultural and political nature, during the early 1900s. In alluding to Kathleen ní Houlihan (one of several allegorical names for Ireland), Seumas reflects the rather superficial knowledge of Irish culture that became common during the period. Once an active member of the Irish Republican Army, Seumas quit in disillusionment with its terrorist policies. But, morally, he is no better than those he condemns for their violence and irresponsibility. When Minnie is arrested, his only fear is that she may get him into trouble. Never once does he see her as the embodiment of the Kathleen ní Houlihan sung about in the old patriotic songs.

In keeping with the satiric portraits, O'Casey gave us of Davoren and Seumas, the other male characters in *The Shadow of a Gunman* are poor in mind and spirit. Landlord Mulligan, who owns the tenement, is a pretentious man who tries to amass wealth at the expense of his impoverished tenants; yet he considers himself a good Irishman. Tommy Owens reveals himself as a clown who sheds tears for Ireland but has never had a gun in his hand nor a sober thought in his head; he is so eager to be associated with the gunmen that he jeopardizes Davoren's life by talking about his presumed rebel activities in a bar.

Mr. Gallogher is also a foolish coward who considers himself a great patriot. The letter he wrote to the rebel government's courts, with its pompous legalisms and misuse of technical terms, is really a device of satire. Gallogher, like many other Irishmen, regarded these courts, originally established to usurp the function of the English courts in Ireland, merely as battlegrounds for petty squabbles among neighbors. The Orangeman

Grigson is a drunk, a bigot, and a coward who ter-
rorizes his mousy little wife but grovels before the
English soldiers when they mock him.

Most of the male characters are caught up in the
rhetoric of dying for Ireland. They speak eloquently of
patriotism, philosophy, religion, poetry, and history.
But their quasi-learned allusions, bombastic words,
and arrogant postures reveal an inner emptiness borne
out by their inability, or unwillingness, to act when the
moment calls for heroic action. The verbal idiosyncra-
sies of these characters are often very amusing to the
audience, but their behavior is not. All of them—not
only Davoren—are mere shadows of the men they pretend to be. Maguire actually does die in an ambush,
but even he is irresponsible for having left the bombs
in Seumas's room.

The female characters in the play have no, or few,
pretensions about themselves; but it is they who take
action when the crucial moment comes. With calm
resolution, Minnie removes the bag of bombs during
the raid. When she is arrested, only Mrs. Henderson
tries to help her. Even Mrs. Grigson, who had been
critical of the flamboyant girl earlier in the play, pities
her tragic death. Minnie's flaw of character, if it can be
described as that, is a romanticism that invests Davoren with qualities a more knowledgeable person
would never attribute to a man so obviously a poseur.

There were, and are, critics who condemned *The
Shadow of a Gunman* for what they considered its
stereotypic characters—like Mrs. Henderson, who
talks in "stage Irish"—and its melodramatic incidents,
such as the bloodied piece of paper on the pathetic
little Minnie's still breast. But what these critics may
have missed was O'Casey's original contribution to the
modern stage. He had juxtaposed stock comedy and
serious ideas in a drama that bore a powerful and
ironic message: the old romantic Ireland was gone.

Kathleen ní Houlihan, who once played the harp and sang to her valiant warriors, had become a grim reaper thanks to the would-be patriots who conducted rebellion with brave songs and boastful phrases—a far cry, indeed, from Ireland's invincibles.

Apparently the people of Dublin were weary of violence by the time *The Shadow of a Gunman* appeared at the Abbey Theatre in 1923. Lady Gregory wrote in her *Journals* (published as *Lady Gregory's Journals*, 1947) that all the political events were "taken up with delight by a big audience." During its initial run, the theater was always packed.

Part of the success of the play lay in its realistic atmosphere and accurate re-creation of the psychological impact of the Anglo-Irish War. In a series of lectures delivered during the Abbey Theatre Festival held in Dublin in 1938 (published in *The Irish Theater*, edited by Lennox Robinson, 1939), the Irish critic Walter Starkie praised O'Casey for his dramatic realism:

> O'Casey makes us see the terrible sufferings of the poor, of the revolutionaries, of those "on the run," and, as usual, the sacrifice of innocent victims. Many of us have lived through that period when the city resounded with the sound of bombs and revolver shots. Late at night we used to be wakened by a loud knock at the door. Then we could hear the throbbing of a motor engine . . . men would rush up . . . nights [were] lit up by flashlights of the lorries [trucks] . . . after "curfew time." . . . All of those scenes appear to us again as we watch *The Shadow of a Gunman.*

In November 1958, *The Shadow of a Gunman* was produced at the Bijou Theater in New York, under the direction of Jack Garfein. It was the first production of the play seen by New Yorkers since the fall of 1932, when the Abbey Theatre repertory company presented it on tour. The critic Brooks Atkinson, of the *New York Times* (21 November 1958), described the play itself as "A Prologue to Greatness" and Garfein's production as a "masterly performance" in which every part was "brilliantly acted." Atkinson observed that the direction of Garfein and the superiority of the Actors Studio players brought vivid life to the script. The setting of the cluttered tenement room and the messy costumes gave the play an unusual visual vitality. And the contrast between the torpid pace of the first act and the tension of the second beautifully varied the pitch of the drama. The sense that one got from the production, Atkinson concluded, was of a turbulent exterior life in which the characters participated when they were not on the stage. He made particular mention of Susan Strasberg's starry-eyed Minnie Powell and of William Smithers's egotistical Davoren.

No other significant production of *The Shadow of a Gunman* appeared in the United States until March 1972, when it was staged in New York at the Sheridan Square Playhouse, Off-Broadway. Clive Barnes, of the *New York Times* (1 March 1972), entitled his review "A Cruelly Topical Play." It was a time when once again Ireland, that is, Northern Ireland, was an armed camp.

Relevant to the times as the play might have been, the production was seriously marred by the limited facilities and amateur cast of the Playhouse. The realistic atmosphere and psychological impact of the original Abbey production, which the play demands, was diminished by the inadequate staging. For example, O'Casey specified in his stage directions a back wall entirely covered by two large windows. Thus, when Davoren and Seumas hear the gunfire, they feel it is as dangerous to be inside as outside—and it is. But the Sheridan Square Playhouse set had only one small window.

The inadequate staging of the production could also be seen in the placement of the religious statuary, the importance of which is symbolic as well as theatrical. In the stage directions, O'Casey specified a Virgin to the right, a Sacred Heart to the left, and a crucifix in the center of a mantelshelf. The arrangement of these votive figures constitutes the only order in the otherwise slovenly life of Seumas, to whom they belong. He worships them virtually as idols, for he evidences no grasp of the moral and ethical values of Christianity, which they represent. The statuary is important to the characterization of Seumas, but in the Playhouse production they were not very noticeable and could have been overlooked by an audience unacquainted with the text of the play.

Brooks Atkinson once pointed out that O'Casey "is the paradox of the theater." Despite his theatrical genius, he is one of the least-performed playwrights in the English-speaking world. And, on the rare occasions when he is performed, the production is often marred by inadequate staging and non-professional actors. The truth is that O'Casey makes exacting demands on his actors, directors, and stage designers. Although the first and in many ways the least complex of O'Casey's dramas, *The Shadow of a Gunman* is no exception to that truth.

Juno and the Paycock

    Juno and the Paycock: A Tragedy in Three Acts, O'Casey's first full-length play, was produced in 1924 at the Abbey Theatre in Dublin. The time of the play is 1922, when the Irish Civil War was being fought over the peace treaty that ended the Anglo-Irish War and, with other parliamentary acts, provided for the division of Ireland into the Irish Free State and Northern Ireland, which remained within the United Kingdom. So-called Free Staters and Republicans, formerly comrades in the Anglo-Irish War, were now bent upon the destruction of one another.

    The plot of *Juno and the Paycock* is comprised of three episodes that end in the dissolution of the Boyle family. A legacy left to the father, "Captain" Boyle, never materializes; the daughter is betrayed by her lover; and the son is murdered by his Republican comrades, who suspect him of having betrayed one of their number to the Free Staters. The title of the play takes its name from the mother, known as "Juno," and her husband, whom she calls a "Paycock" (the Irish pronunciation of "peacock"). The title also suggests the Roman goddess Juno, whose symbol in classical mythology is the peacock; she, like her Irish namesake, is also bedeviled by an erring husband, Jupiter.

All three acts of the play take place in the living room of a two-room apartment belonging to the Boyles. To the left is a door leading to the second room; there is a window next to it. At the back is a dresser on which some books are visible. Leaning against the dresser is a long-handled shovel used by laborers when turning concrete or mixing mortar. Farther to the right is another window with a tiny outside porch. Between the right window and the dresser is a picture of the Virgin. Below the picture, on a bracket, is a crimson bowl that contains a burning votive light. Also to the right is a small bed, concealed in part by cretonne curtains strung on twine, and a fireplace with a box of coal. In the first act, a few battered chairs stand near a table on which are the remains of breakfast. There is also a book on the table.

In the published edition of *Juno and the Paycock* (1925), O'Casey described the characters in depth as they appear onstage. Of Mary, the attractive young daughter who is onstage when the curtain rises, he wrote: "Two forces are working in her mind, one through the circumstances of her life, pulling her back; the other, through the influence of books she has read, pushing her forward." Mary is arranging her hair in front of a mirror. Her younger brother, Johnny, who has only one arm, sits crouched beside the fireplace. O'Casey described him as a thin, delicate young man with a pale face and "a tremulous look of indefinite fear in his eyes."

Mary begins to read aloud from a newspaper about Robbie Tancred, a young Republican neighbor who has been found shot to death, apparently the victim of hostile Free Staters. As she reads, their mother Juno appears, carrying some parcels. Once a pretty woman, she now has "a look of listless monotony and harassed anxiety, blending with an expression of mechanical resistance" typical of the working class.

Mary continues describing the gory details of Tancred's murder until her brother insists she stop. Juno has returned from work to prepare her husband's breakfast, and to prevent him from loafing around the apartment all day with his friend Joxer. Boyle should be looking for a job because no one in the family is working except Juno. Mary and her union have gone on strike in sympathy with a fellow worker unfairly dismissed. Juno contends that none of the workers can afford to walk out. But Mary insists that the trade-union principle of solidarity must be supported, no matter what the individual cost.

As they talk, Johnny limps in and out of the room. Juno is worried about him. She speaks of the hip wound he received during the Easter Rebellion, and of the loss of his arm recently when he fought with the Republicans in the civil war. Johnny, exceedingly nervous and troubled, refuses to be left alone in the apartment. And he insists that the votive candle under the picture of the Virgin be kept burning constantly.

Jerry Devine, Mary's former boyfriend, enters the room. O'Casey wrote of him that he is a type that was becoming common in the labor movement, a man smart enough to make his fellow workers into a political power but too ignorant "to broaden that power for the benefit of all." Jerry wants to tell Boyle that Father Farrell, the local priest, has found work for him. Juno sends Jerry to look for her husband in the nearby pub. But she is convinced that Boyle will lose the job intentionally; and she will have to go on, she says, "killin' meself workin', an' he sthruttin' about from mornin' till night like a paycock [peacock]."

Voices can be heard on the stairs, and Mary and Johnny retire into the room offstage. Boyle and Joxer enter. Boyle walks in a "slow, consequential strut," "the upper part of his body slightly thrown back, and his stomach slightly thrust forward." His buddy Joxer

Daly has a wrinkled face with cunning eyes and a grinning mouth; his shoulders constantly shrug and twist. The two men enter the room, complaining about Juno. She suddenly appears before them, and Joxer hurries out.

Juno accuses Boyle of pomposity and falsehood. He assumed, she says, the title of "Captain" after having sailed only once in his life as an ordinary seaman on a collier from Dublin to Liverpool. When Juno informs Boyle of the job awaiting him, he complains of the "cripplin'" pains in his legs. Juno does not believe him. Jerry returns and Boyle berates him for seeking him in the pub. In disgust, Jerry leaves with Mary and Juno.

A thundering knock at the door frightens Johnny, but it is only Joxer, who has seen Juno leave. Joxer notices the books lying around the room. Boyle dismisses them as children's trash that Mary is reading. (They are plays by Ibsen: *The Doll's House, The Wild Duck*, and *Ghosts*.) Boyle begins to boast about the days he spent sailing on the sea, but both men are nervous lest Juno return and find them loafing together. When they do hear her on the stairs, Joxer climbs out of the window onto a little porch where he hides. Juno comes rushing in and tells Boyle that soon he will hear some good news.

Mary and her new boyfriend Charlie Bentham enter. Bentham is a schoolteacher who is studying law in his spare time. He carries gloves and a walking cane—with an air of self-importance. Juno introduces her son to Bentham, explaining that he was maimed during the recent fighting. Boastfully, Johnny dismisses his ill-fortune by insisting that he fought on "principle." Juno comments that he lost his "best" principle when he lost his working arm.

Boyle tells Bentham that he nicknamed his wife "Juno" because she was born, christened, met and married him, and gave birth to Johnny during the month of June. (He fails to mention that Mary was also born in June.) Finally, Bentham gets the opportunity to tell Boyle of a legacy he is to inherit from a deceased cousin. (Bentham wrote the will for the deceased.) Boyle, in astonishment, praises God for his munificence and promises that he will be a changed man. He denounces Joxer as a "prognosticator an' procrastinator." Joxer, who has been hiding on the porch, climbs angrily into the room and denounces Boyle as a pompous old liar. The act ends with an ecstatic Boyle singing affectionately: "Me own, me darlin' Juno, you're all the world to me."

Act II opens on a scene of festivity. New furnishings are everywhere. More furniture is onstage than in the previous act, cheap pictures and photographs now decorate the walls, and huge vases of artificial flowers stand in various corners. Crossed festoons of colored paper hang on the walls in preparation for a party celebrating the forthcoming legacy.

Boyle, half asleep, is stretched out on a couch. Joxer walks in cautiously for fear of meeting Juno; but Boyle grandly invites him in with the declaration that Juno is not the master of the house. Boyle says that he has been busy signing "documents" (IOU's) for money borrowed from the neighbors, to be repaid when the legacy arrives. Juno and Mary walk in, carrying a new gramophone. Juno expresses some concern over the amount of borrowed money the family is spending, but Boyle assures her that the legacy will be more than enough.

Bentham arrives to help celebrate the family's good fortune. Boyle tries to engage Bentham in serious conversation but often finds himself at a loss for words. His favorite observation is that "the whole counthry's in a state o' chassis [chaos]." Juno agrees with him and suggests that the chaos exists because the Irish have not observed their religion better.

Deferentially, Juno asks Bentham for his opinion. He refuses to answer because, unlike the others, he is not a Catholic; he is a Theosophist. At a loss, Juno asks if he believes in ghosts. Mary dismisses the query as preposterous, but Bentham retorts that some people may actually see ghosts. A sensational act such as murder, he believes, demands great energy that may continue to linger at its site. Someone who has a peculiar connection with the energy may thus be able to reconstruct the whole incident.

Their conversation frightens Johnny, who goes into the other room. But he rushes back immediately, screaming that he has seen the dead Robbie Tancred kneeling before the statue of the Virgin. Juno tries to convince him that he is mistaken. In the midst of the confusion, Joxer and Mrs. Maisie Madigan, an upstairs neighbor, arrive for the celebration.

Outside the apartment, people can be heard coming slowly down the stairs. One of the voices is that of Mrs. Tancred, another upstairs neighbor, who is praying to the Blessed Virgin for her son Robbie. Juno suddenly remembers that today is his funeral. When she explains to Bentham that Robbie was a Die Hard (another name for a Republican) and a friend of her son, Johnny objects that they were never friends. Juno regrets not having remembered the funeral, but Boyle tells her testily that they have nothing to do with the government's business. She agrees with Boyle that perhaps Mrs. Tancred got "what she deserved" for permitting her son to hold Republican activities in her home.

Mary and Bentham leave the party, which continues noisily. The tailor "Needle" Nugent walks in and scolds the Boyles for disregarding the Tancred funeral procession, now passing by on the street. The marchers can be heard singing a hymn of brotherly love. All the people at the party except Johnny leave to see the procession. An Irregular (also a name for a Republican) enters the room and demands that Johnny accompany him to a meeting. He suggests ominously that Johnny may have information about Tancred's death. Terrified, Johnny refuses to move, and the Irregular leaves with a sinister warning. Outside, the mourners can be heard chanting "Hail, Mary, full of grace." Inside the room, Johnny cringes in a corner.

Act III takes place about two months later. Mary is sitting by the fireplace. Juno asks if Bentham has written her since his unexpected departure for England. She replies that he has not. Mary looks so ill that Juno insists she see a doctor. Boyle is lying on the bed behind the cretonne curtains. Juno scolds him for not going to the lawyer's to find out why the legacy has been delayed, and Boyle answers irritably that he has already inquired many times with no success.

After the women leave to see the doctor, Joxer and the tailor enter the room. Boyle, who is still on the bed, does not hear them come in, nor can he hear their conversation, which is conducted in loud whispers. According to Joxer, the Boyles will never get the legacy. Bentham made a mistake in writing the will; he failed to specify the name of Boyle as the cousin who was to inherit the legacy and, as a consequence, hundreds of "cousins" have appeared in the lawyer's office to claim their share. The tailor leaves quietly after taking from a chair a suit he made for Boyle on credit.

Boyle finally rouses himself. Before leaving, Joxer tells him that people suspect there will be no inheritance. Johnny, who has been in the other room, enters just as Juno returns. She tells them that Mary is pregnant and has been abandoned by Bentham. Boyle threatens to throw Mary out of the house, but Juno warns him that she too will leave if Mary is forced to go.

Juno suggests that the family find another apartment once the money comes so that their friends will not be aware of Mary's condition. Boyle admits he has known for a long time that the legacy will never come because of a mistake Bentham made. Taken to task by Johnny for having borrowed money he knew he could not repay, Boyle leaves the apartment to use his last few coins for a drink.

Two movers arrive to repossess the unpaid furniture and begin carrying it out. Juno goes to look for Boyle so that he can stop them. Mary enters, followed a few minutes later by Jerry. He has learned from Juno of Bentham's departure and pleads with Mary to return to him. When Mary tells him she is pregnant, however, he reneges on his offer and hurries off. Johnny attacks Mary for telling Jerry, who might have helped them, about her pregnancy. In despair, Mary flees from the apartment. The movers pick up a chest of drawers and the votive light on top flickers out. Johnny screams in terror, for he believes his continued safety depends on the burning light.

Two Irregulars with drawn revolvers appear and order Johnny to go with them; he has been formally accused by the Republicans of having betrayed Robbie Tancred to the Free Staters.

Johnny pleads with them: "I'm an oul' comrade—yous wouldn't shoot an oul' comrade. . . . Are yous goin' to do in a comrade?—look at me arm, I lost it for Ireland." The Irregulars tell Johnny to get his rosary and drag him off as he prays to the Sacred Heart of Jesus.

The curtain falls for a few minutes to indicate the passage of an hour or so. It rises on a room completely empty of furniture. Mary and Juno have just heard from neighbors that Johnny was forcibly taken away by two men with guns. Mrs. Madigan enters. She says that the police waiting below have found Johnny's body riddled with bullets, and they want Juno to go with them to the station to identify it.

In an anguished voice, Juno tells Mary that they will leave the apartment, together, forever. She knows now that Boyle is hopeless. They will work for the sake of Mary's unborn child. Mary is dejected because the child will have no father, but Juno assures her it will have what is even better—two mothers.

As Juno leaves to identify the dead body at the police station, she expresses guilt for not having been more sympathetic to Mrs. Tancred when Robbie was killed. She feels she should have remembered only that Robbie was a "poor, dead son," not that he was a Republican Die-Hard. And she quotes from memory the prayer of Mrs. Tancred as she walked down the stairs past the Boyle apartment to attend Robbie's funeral. Whether their sons were Republicans or Free Staters, concludes Juno, a mother's grief is always the same. Juno, Mary, and Mrs. Madigan walk out of the room slowly.

For a few moments the stage is empty. Then Joxer and Boyle reel in, staggeringly drunk. As he sinks down slowly Boyle cries out that the country will have to "settle" itself. Now sprawled out on the floor, Boyle mutters his oft-repeated observation that "th' whole worl's . . . in a terr . . . ible state o' . . . chassis!" The final curtain descends.

On the whole, the response to *Juno and the Paycock* was enthusiastic. There were a few important critics, however, who questioned O'Casey's ability as a theatrical craftsman. According to them, he often used incidents or devices simply because they fit his preconceived purpose, not because they developed naturally from plot or characterization. His reference to the dramas of Ibsen was cited as an example because they are presumably irrelevant to the overall drama.

In Act I, Boyle denigrates Mary for reading what he calls "chiselurs' thrash" ("children's trash") like *The Wild Duck, The Doll's House,* and *Ghosts.* Boyle obviously does not recognize Ibsen's name as that of a great dramatist. These dramas, however, have specific meaning in the characterization of Mary, described by O'Casey as a girl whose reading has helped to push her forward out of the impoverished circumstances of her life. And the dramas also foreshadow developments in the plot. Mary's childish illusions about Jerry and Bentham (men who claim to live for their ideals) will be destroyed by their behavior, just as the innocent child Hedvig, in *The Wild Duck,* is destroyed by Gregers Werle in his pursuit of ideal truth. Mary and Juno, like Nora in *The Doll's House,* will walk away from a man they consider hopeless in order to fend for themselves. And the weak Johnny, a victim of society, will die, doomed by the ghost of Robbie Tancred; he is comparable to Oswald Elving in *Ghosts,* who also dies a victim of ghosts from the past. Pathetic, both young men leave behind them mothers who, in their terrible, but ennobling, grief, become heroic figures of tragedy.

In addition to Ibsen's dramas, unsympathetic critics have cited Bentham's theosophy as another of O'Casey's irrelevancies. Theosophy, little known or practiced by Irishmen of the 1920s, is a type of religious speculation dealing with the mystical apprehension of God, associated with various occult systems and often incorporating aspects of Buddhism and Brahmanism. But Bentham's esoteric religious beliefs are very much of a piece with his unusual dress—the gloves and the cane—all indicative of his good opinion of himself. When Bentham tries to explain theosophy to Juno (Act II), his discussion of ghosts results in Johnny's horrifying vision of the dead Robbie Tancred, kneeling before the statue of the Virgin. Thus, Boyle's mention of Ibsen's *Ghosts* in Act I prefigures an episode that occurs in Act II.

With regard to the drawing of character, however, virtually everyone including the critics agreed that O'Casey was a master craftsman. "The Paycock" and Juno are considered two of the greatest feats of characterization through language of the modern stage. O'Casey's familiarity with the Elizabethan dramatists, Shakespeare in particular, and the King James Version of the Bible is evident in their dialogue—in its daring, recklessness, humor; in its richness, profusion, grandeur; in its sincerity, intensity, eloquence; and ultimately in its grand human appeal.

The Shakespearean speech of Boyle is sweeping and colorful with an underlay of sarcasm, humorous in effect. In the following quotation, Boyle is scolding Jerry for seeking him in the pub to deliver Father Farrell's message about a job:

> What do you want to be gallopin' about afther me for? Is a man not to be allowed to leave his house for a minute without havin' a pack o' spies, pimps an' informers cantherin' at his heels? . . . I don't want the motions of me body to be watched the way an asthronomer ud watch a star.

Boyle continues to complain about Father Farrell's interest in getting him a job:

> Father Farrell's beginnin' to take a great intherest in Captain Boyle; because of what Johnny did for his country, says he to me wan day. It's a curious way to reward Johnny be makin' his poor oul' father work. . . . Job! Well, let him give his job to wan of his hymn-singin', prayer-spoutin', crawthumpin' Confraternity men [a religious lay order]!

Boyle's Falstaffian speech characterizes him as intractable, irritable, bombastic, and amusing. Also like Falstaff, the old fat knight, Boyle is cast in the mold of the *miles gloriosus* of classical comedy—the bragging, swaggering soldier—now transformed into a drunken Irishman.

Often, critics have described Boyle as a "charming" rascal, difficult to hate even at the end of the play. But there is another reading of his character. O'Casey drew him with surface charm, in large part through his comic speech; and he succeeded in maintaining that surface, while surrounding Boyle with the despair of the other members of the family, until the tragic ending of the play. But the villainy in Boyle was suggested by O'Casey from the moment he walks on stage.

Boyle is the center of his own universe, a blusterer whose pride far surpasses his merit. While his family sinks slowly into tragedy, the "Paycock," with his "consequential strut," evades the opportunity to work by pretending illness, fabricates stories of heroism about himself, and storms out when confronted with his own lies. He mocks his daughter for her attempts at self-improvement, denounces his wife for wanting him to get a job, and dismisses his son, who is in a constant state of terror. Now pompous, now querulous, Boyle is always wise in his own conceit, and his family pays dearly for his vanity.

Boyle looks out on a world that, for him, is always "unsettled." In the last scene of the play, when he staggers in from the pub and sinks down on the floor, his comic mask is ripped away by O'Casey to reveal the brutal face beneath. We see the ignorance and pretension of a lazy, mean scoundrel and liar who reeks of moral turpitude. When betrayal, hatred, terror, and bloodshed have emptied his home, the sodden Boyle declares solemnly that "th' whole worl's in a terrible state o' chassis!" with unintentional self-mockery. He is the comic miscreant in hell.

Boyle's grotesque figure is contrasted by Juno as the mother figure who becomes the tragic muse. Like Boyle, Juno sometimes speaks with an Elizabethan profusion and humor, particularly when she complains about him. Basically, however, her speech, like her character, is moderate, straightforward, and sensible. But she has the great biblically inspired monologue near the end of Act III. The circumstances are heartbreaking: her lazy husband is out drinking; her foolish daughter has been abandoned by a snob; and her sniveling son has been murdered by the Republicans. Juno criticizes herself for not having been sorry enough for Mrs. Tancred when her son Robbie was killed. She remembers and repeats the prayer of Mrs. Tancred on the way to his funeral, with a significant difference. Mrs. Tancred had prayed for the Mother of God to "have pity on the pair of us"—herself and Mrs. Mannin', whose Free State son had been killed in an ambush led by Robbie. Juno prays for "pity on us all": by her total compassion, which is an integral part of her character, Juno acquires universal dimension. As she leaves to identify Johnny's body at the police station, Juno laments:

> What was the pain I suffered, Johnny, bringin' you into the world to carry you to your cradle, to the pains I'll suffer carryin' you out o' the world to bring you to your grave! Mother o' God, Mother o' God, have pity on us all! Blessed Virgin, where were you when me darlin' son was riddled with bullets, when me darlin' son was riddled with bullets? Sacred Heart o' Jesus, take away our hearts o' stone, and give us hearts o' flesh! Take away this murdherin' hate, and give us Thine own eternal love.

O'Casey achieved Juno's song of lamentation, an authentic maternal threnody, by fusing the Dublin idiom with lines from the Old Testament prophet Ezekiel and from the Roman Catholic litanies of "The Most Sacred Heart of Jesus" and "The Blessed Virgin."

From the popular speech of Dublin, known as Anglo-Irish, O'Casey took over vocabulary, morphology, syntax, phonetic characteristics, and speaking rhythm. Dublin speech possesses long, rhythmical cadences of a musical modulation and colorful, emotional imagery very close to the poetical language of the King James Version of the Bible.

O'Casey's use, therefore, of lines from Ezekiel for Juno's threnody is quite compatible with Dublin speech, as the original passage from Ezekiel indicates:

> And I will give them one heart, and I will put a new spirit within you; and I will take the stony heart out of their flesh, and I will give them a heart of flesh.
>
> Ezekiel 11:19

With these lines, O'Casey interspersed allusions to the Sacred Heart of Jesus, the Blessed Virgin, and the Mother of God from Roman-Catholic litanies. The use of such religious terminology by Juno is quite consistent with her Catholicism.

Despite the highly rhetorical structure of Juno's threnody, its words are simple, its statement direct, its intensity of feeling authentic, and its effect sublime. The threnody reflects O'Casey's deep admiration for Irish womanhood. Juno stands forth as a symbol of faith, loyalty, courage, and charity. It is she alone who points out the hopelessness of living by abstract principles that are destructive to human life, as in the case of Mary's sentimental attitude about the strike or Johnny's boastfulness about the loss of his arm. It is she alone who condemns the ideologues of all political faiths for the terror they have inflicted on the people. It is she alone who tries to steady the tottering world of the Boyle family. Juno is O'Casey's apotheosis of the figure of the mother, based on his image of his own mother. With her song of lamentation, Juno takes on the stature of a tragic muse.

Several themes related to the general condition of Ireland are implicit in the dramatic action of *Juno and the Paycock*. Often, they reflect O'Casey's increasing disillusionment with the new Free State government.

One of O'Casey's main themes is a condemnation of both the Republicans and the Free Staters for their brutality toward one another. For the sake of political "principle," young men like Robbie Tancred and Johnny Boyle are entrapped in an unending round of sadism coupled with murder. One irony is heaped upon another by O'Casey in the play. Johnny's involvement in the political scene was based more upon his youthful vanity than upon any strong commitment to the ideals and values of republicanism. Men who were once comrades torture one another and yet continue to think of themselves as good Roman Catholics. And they call upon the holy saints to help them in their murdering hate.

Bitter criticism of the middle class, which dominated the Free State government, is another theme implicit in the play. The elusive inheritance of the Boyle family may symbolize the illusory hopes of the common people under the Free State. Blinded by the prospect of ready money, the family goes into debt for tawdry goods and suddenly becomes politically conservative as well as calloused toward others who do not share their views. Even Juno buys on excessive credit and speaks unkindly of Mrs. Tancred for permitting Republican activities in her home.

O'Casey regarded the pledge of the Free State gov-

ernment for the welfare of the common people as illusory as the Boyle inheritance. Soon after the founding of the Free State, a new middle class of petite
bourgeoisie—middlemen, importers, small manufac-
turers—either arose or entrenched itself more firmly in
positions of power. This class comprised neither intellectuals nor the proletariat that were consistently
O'Casey's focus. In the few instances where members
of the working class did become officials of the government, they soon lost their sense of working-class
identity.

According to O'Casey, the middle class, by 1922, not
only had complete control of the Free State government but also had usurped even the Republican movement for its own profit. They had laid low the concept
of the common task and the common good. The principles of men such as Parnell remained forever elusive
in a morally and spiritually bankrupt Ireland. And the
common people were worse off than before.

Within this context of a morally and spiritually
bankrupt Ireland, Boyle's much reiterated phrase—"th'
whole worl's in a state o' chassis"—takes on multiple
meanings. It begins as a gag line, restricted to Boyle's
idiosyncratic mode of talk. Then it takes on relevance
in terms of the chaotic situation that is developing in
the Boyle family. Finally, the chaos, social as well as
spiritual, which destroys the family unit becomes symbolic of an Ireland caught in the throes of fratricide. It
is another instance of O'Casey's artistry that Boyle's
gag line gives universal implication to the dramatic
action, just as Juno's lamentation for Johnny univer-
salizes her experience into a plea for every mother
bereft of child.

Juno and the Paycock premiered on 3 March 1924 at
the Abbey Theatre. As Lady Gregory wrote in her
Journals, the run of the play was extended so that

those who were turned away from the crowded theater could be accommodated the following week.
Barry Fitzgerald and Sara Allgood, members of the
Abbey Theatre company, were magnificent as Boyle
and Juno. Fitzgerald himself was more impressed by
Juno and Paycock than by any other in which he had
previously acted. It was, he said many years later, "a
terrific experience," and the only time on stage that he
ever felt "an enormous influence coming from behind"
(*New York Times*, 14 January 1940).

After a successful Dublin run, the play was produced in November 1925 at the Royalty Theatre in
London with Arthur Sinclair as Boyle and Sara Allgood as Juno. During its long run, the reviews were
mainly favorable. A year later, O'Casey was invited to
London to receive the Hawthornden prize for that
play.

In the years 1927, 1931, and 1934, the Abbey Theatre repertory company toured the United States and
parts of Canada. *Juno and the Paycock* was one of the
plays most in demand. Unfortunately, on none of these
tours did audiences have the opportunity of seeing
both Fitzgerald and Allgood together in the title roles,
although the actors who replaced one or the other
were considered very good.

In January 1940, however, Fitzgerald and Allgood
appeared together for the first time in this country
with the Abbey Theatre repertory company. Their
performance was one of the highlights of theatrical
history. Virtually every critic unstintingly admired
them. Brooks Atkinson, of the *New York Times* (17
January 1940), was ecstatic in his praise: "Count it as
a dispensation to have two such glorious actors as Miss
Allgood and Mr. Fitzgerald in immortal parts that suit
them."

Atkinson wrote that Fitzgerald would never have a
richer part, for the character of Boyle can never be

drawn again. Although Atkinson considered Juno's role less spectacular than Boyle's, he felt Miss Allgood's interpretation was also masterful. In the final tragic scene, he described her as conveying superbly the anguish that more than any other emotion dominates the action. In Atkinson's view, Miss Allgood "may well be proud of the honesty and skill of this bustling portrait of a mother against whom the black world she knows has pitilessly conspired."

In a follow-up article (28 January 1940), Atkinson concluded that someday, somewhere, some young people would be thinking enviously of the time when O'Casey was writing mighty plays and Fitzgerald and Allgood were around to act them. The first half of the twentieth century would seem like a golden age and he advised New York audiences to appreciate such occasions when they happened.

Fitzgerald and Allgood have died since Atkinson wrote those words. Although the play has been produced by American companies in the United States several times since the famous 1940 tour, no actor or actress playing the title roles has ever received such praise as the original performers. It may be that *Juno and the Paycock* demands an Irish cast of professionals for the sake of O'Casey's glorious, Anglo-Irish language.

The Plough and the Stars

The Plough and the Stars: A Tragedy in Four Acts was produced in 1926 at the Abbey Theatre in Dublin. Acts I and II occur in November 1915, a period during which various Irish organizations were preparing to overthrow the English government in Ireland.

Frequently political rallies with well-known militant orators were held. Acts III and IV take place during the Easter Rebellion, 1916, when Dublin was set afire by English shells and thousands of innocent civilians were either wounded or killed in the cross fire between the government forces and the Irish rebels.

The plot of *The Plough and the Stars* shows the impact of the Rebellion upon the lives of the rebels and neutral Dubliners trapped in the conflict. The title is taken from the flag of the Irish Citizen Army, one of the paramilitary organizations that fought in the Rebellion. O'Casey described the flag in his third autobiographical volume, *Drums under the Windows:*

> There it was—the most beautiful flag among the flags of the world's nations; a rich, deep poplin field of blue; across its whole length and breadth

stretched the formalised shape of a plough, a golden-brown colour, seamed with a rusty red, while through all glittered the gorgeous group of stars enriching and ennobling the northern skies.

Act I is set in the front room of what was once a fine, old Georgian mansion but is now a Dublin tenement slum. O'Casey wrote in his stage directions that the room "is furnished in a way that suggests an attempt towards a finer expression of domestic life." A casement cloth of a dark purple, decorated with a design in reddish purple and cream, drapes the space originally occupied by folding doors.

Four reproductions hang on the walls: over a clock on the mantelshelf is "The Sleeping Venus," by Giorgione; on the chimney, a portrait of Robert Emmet, a famous eighteenth-century Irish patriot; and at the back entrance, on either side, "The Gleaners" and "The Angelus," by Jean François Millet. Underneath "The Gleaners" is a chest of drawers on which a green bowl filled with scarlet dahlias and white chrysanthemums stands.

On top of a gate-leg table, placed opposite the fireplace, to the right, is a huge cavalry sword. Next to the table is a door that leads to the lobby of the tenement. The flame of a gaslamp can be seen through the window at the back; it gives light to workmen who are repairing the streets outside. (Occasionally the clang of their crowbars can be heard.)

The tenants who occupy the room are the newlyweds Jack and Nora Clitheroe, her Uncle Peter, and Jack's cousin, whose nickname is The Covey. As the curtain rises, Fluther Good, a carpenter who also lives in the tenement, is fixing the lock on the lobby door of the Clitheroe apartment. As described by O'Casey, Fluther is a man of forty years, "rarely surrendering to thoughts of anxiety, fond of his 'oil' [liquor] but determined to conquer the habit before he dies." Peter is sitting near the fire, drying a fancy white shirt. He is an irritable, thin little man with a straggly, wiry beard.

Outside the apartment door, Mrs. Gogan, who also lives in the tenement, can be heard accepting a delivery for Nora. She walks in with the package. Mrs. Gogan, the mother of a consumptive girl named Mollser and a new-born child, is a doleful little woman of forty—fidgety, nervous, terribly talkative, and aflame with curiosity. She begins wandering about, picking up whatever thing is near her, and fiddling with it. She annoys Peter, who marches in and out of the room angrily. He becomes particularly incensed when she touches the fancy white shirt and calvary sword that belong to him. They are part of the dress uniform of the Foresters, a patriotic Irish organization to which Peter belongs. He plans to wear them that evening at a public rally for Irish independence.

We learn from the conversation of Mrs. Gogan and Fluther that the Clitheroes, although recently married, are having problems. According to Mrs. Gogan, Clitheroe has cooled toward his wife because of his absorbing interest in the Irish Citizen Army, of which he was a member until recently. Nora, in turn, is very antagonistic toward her husband's political interests.

The noise of the workmen outside the apartment is suddenly interrupted by a cheer; then, there is the clang of tools being dropped, followed by silence. The Covey enters the room. O'Casey said of him: "He is about twenty-five, tall, thin, with lines on his face that form a perpetual protest against life as he conceives it to be."

Mrs. Gogan asks The Covey what has happened to the workmen outside. He replies in disgust that they have been mobilized to march under the flag of the Irish Citizen Army at the rally that evening. A socialist, The Covey insists that the workers are disgracing the Plough and the Stars by introducing it into a nationalistic rally; the flag should be unfurled only when the people are establishing a workers' republic, not an Irish republic. The Covey begins to bait Peter about his fancy Forester uniform. Peter becomes so incensed he lunges at him with the cavalry sword just as Nora walks in.

O'Casey described Nora in some detail:

> She is a young woman of twenty-two, alert, swift, full of nervous energy, and a little anxious to get on in the world. The firm lines of her face are considerably opposed by a soft, amorous mouth and gentle eyes. When her firmness fails her, she persuades with her feminine charm.

Nora accuses The Covey and Peter of undermining whatever respectability she has tried to maintain in their apartment.

Bessie Burgess, an upstairs neighbor, appears in the open doorway. She is a vigorously built woman of about forty with a face hardened by work and coarsened by drink. (Unlike her neighbors, Bessie is a Protestant and loyal to the government of England.) She upbraids Nora for her pretensions to gentility and particularly resents Nora's complaints about her singing of hymns at night when she has had a few drinks. Grabbing the younger woman, Bessie threatens to "paste" her in the face, but Fluther pulls them apart.

During the fracas, Clitheroe enters, a tall, muscular fellow of about twenty-five. His face has none of the strength of Nora's; it is a face in which there is the desire for authority but none of the power to obtain it. Clitheroe bodily shoves Bessie out of the apartment. She protests that were her son home from the trenches in France—he is fighting in the English Army in the war against Germany—he would right the wrongs being done her.

Nora prepares the table for family tea after Mrs. Gogan and Fluther leave. Clitheroe would like to attend the rally that night, but Nora refuses to go. The Covey announces sarcastically that he plans to go "to have a look at Ireland's warriors passin' by," an obvious jibe at Forester Peter.

Peter and The Covey leave for the rally. Once the young couple is alone, Nora tries to be intimate with her husband, but both are edgy. When Clitheroe insists that he quit the Irish Citizen Army because of her, Nora laughingly recalls that he had also failed to get his expected promotion to captain. Clitheroe accuses her of being "snotty." Nora reminds him of their earlier, happier days of lovemaking. But they are interrupted by Captain Brennan, of the Irish Citizen Army, with a message from General "Jim" Connolly. Clitheroe learns that he had in fact been promoted to captain and that Nora burned the letter bearing the news. Furious with her deception, he leaves for the rally with Brennan.

The unhappy Nora is joined by Mollser, the consumptive daughter of Mrs. Gogan. She has come to visit Nora because her mother has gone to the rally and she fears dying alone. Mollser calls Nora's attention to the music of a brass band heard in the distance; it is accompanying a regiment of Irish soldiers to the boat that will take them to the Western Front. As the regiment swings into the street by the Clitheroe apartment, the soldiers can be heard singing "It's a Long Way to Tipperary."

Nora and Mollser sit listening quietly but are startled by the unexpected appearance of Bessie in the darkened, open doorway. She warns them that doom awaits the Irish nationalists and their families as well.

Act II is set in a "public house" (what Americans

would call a bar) at the corner of the street where the rally is being held. One corner of the barroom is visible to the audience. On the back wall is a large, two-paned window, which is somewhat opaque. Next to it, on the right, are swinging doors that lead to a small, private room. Outside, through the large window, can be seen the faint outlines of a platform; it is occupied by one of the speakers at the rally.

The bartender is wiping some glasses, while Rosie, a prostitute, stands nearby toying with a half-empty glass. She is a pert, pretty girl dressed in a low-cut blouse and skirt. Rosie, who is not getting any customers this evening, takes a jaundiced view of the men at the rally: "You'd think they were th' glorious company of th' saints, an' th' noble army of martyrs thrampin' through th' sthreets o' paradise."

A man standing on the platform outside can be heard addressing the rally. (O'Casey refers to him in the cast of characters as "The Figure in the Window"; hereafter he will be referred to as The Figure.) The Figure, whose enlarged shadow is framed by the opaque window, calls upon his fellow Irishmen to take up arms against the English tyrants. As The Figure moves away to speak to the people at the right of the platform, his shadow diminishes in size until he can no longer be seen or heard by the audience in the theater.

Rosie and the bartender, agree that The Figure has spoken the "sacred thruth [truth]" about the need for Irish independence. Peter and Fluther, both highly excited by the speech they have also just heard, rush into the bar for a drink. They vie with one another in expressing their love for Ireland. The Figure again moves into view and stops in the middle of the platform. Addressing his words to the "Comrade Soldiers of the Irish Volunteers and of the Citizen Army," The Figure embraces the idea of national redemption through the shedding of Irish blood for the cause of independence. In order to hear The Figure better, Fluther and Peter rush out of the bar.

The Covey enters, and Rosie, in hope of some business, begins a conversation with him. He lectures her on the futility of the rally outside unless political freedom is accompanied by economic freedom. Rosie agrees, but when she sidles up to him and puts her arm around his neck, The Covey panics. He runs out of the bar, shouting that he wants nothing to do "with a lassie like you."

Peter and Fluther return with Mrs. Gogan, who carries her baby in her arms. They are followed by The Covey and Bessie, both of whom are antagonistic toward the rally. Bessie and Mrs. Gogan trade insults about religion and politics until they are interrupted by The Figure, whose shadow is again visible through the window. His voice can be heard speaking passionately about "the exhilaration of war," which Ireland must welcome as she would welcome the Angel of God.

The Figure passes out of sight and hearing, and the two women, who by now are somewhat drunk, renew their quarrel even more violently than before. It ends with Bessie's accusing Mrs. Gogan of decorating her finger with a wedding ring but being "hard put" to show her marriage certificate. In a frenzy, Mrs. Gogan shouts that any child of hers, living or dead, "was got between th' bordhers of th' Ten Commandments." Despite the attempts of the men to pacify them, Mrs. Gogan shoves her infant into Peter's unwilling arms and tries to hit Bessie, who is also in a fighting stance. The bartender pushes the women out of doors, and Peter, with the baby in his arms, tears after them.

The Covey, Rosie, and Fluther remain at the bar. When The Covey dismisses the rally as "a lot o' blasted nonsense," Fluther protests and points to the scar on his head, left by the saber of an English soldier during a nationalist rally some years ago. The Covey, unimpressed, says that Fluther has no working-class identity, an idea that so enrages Fluther he threatens to punch him. To avoid trouble, the bartender pushes The Covey into the street also.

By this time quite drunk, Fluther disappears with Rosie into the private little room next to the bar. Just as they exit, Captain Brennan, Lieutenant Langon, and Clitheroe enter hurriedly. Brennan carries the Plough and the Stars; Langon carries the green, white, and orange tricolor of the Irish Volunteers. O'Casey described their appearance:

> *They are in a state of emotional excitement. Their faces are flushed and their eyes sparkle; they speak rapidly, as if unaware of the meaning of what they said. They have been mesmerized by the fervency of the speeches.*

Brennan, Langon, and Clitheroe begin to speak of the need for revolution even to the death: Ireland is greater than mother or wife. They are interrupted by The Figure, whose preternaturally large shadow is seen through the bar window for the fourth and final time. The Figure disparages the foes of an Ireland they think is pacified; the fools have forgotten that the "unfree" graves of the Fenian dead will never leave the young men of Ireland at peace. Brennan, Langon, and Clitheroe pledge themselves to imprisonment, wounds, or death for the "Independence of Ireland." They hurry out to the rally as the bugle blows the assembly.

Rosie and Fluther, both now very drunk, come gaily out from the little room. As they stumble to Rosie's apartment, arm in arm, she sings a risqué song about the love of a sailor and his girl. Outside the bar,

Clitheroe's abrupt command to the Irish Citizen Army to march can be heard as the curtain descends.

Act III takes place six months later, during the week of the Easter Rebellion, outside the Clitheroe tenement. A long, gaunt, five-story building, its brick front is chipped and scarred by age. All the windows are grimy and draped with soiled lace curtains except the two of the Clitheroe room, which are hung with casement cloth.

As the house is revealed, Mrs. Gogan is helping her consumptive daughter Mollser, who can hardly move, into a chair next to the tenement. Mrs. Gogan complains of the shooting in the streets that kept her awake all night. (The people are not yet aware of the extent of the Rebellion.) She says that Fluther went out in the middle of the night looking for Nora, who had tried to follow her husband when he left to join the rebels.

The Covey and Peter come onstage with news of the fighting that rages in the center of the city, where the rebels are occupying the General Post Office. The Covey reports that General Pearse, with his staff nearby, read a proclamation declaring the Irish Republic. Peter adds that the English gunboat Helga is shelling Liberty Hall (the headquarters of the Irish Citizen Army).

Fluther appears supporting the exhausted Nora, now several months pregnant. Nora tells the others that rebels shamed her for her behavior and refused to tell where Clitheroe was. Nora describes the dead and twisted bodies in the streets; she curses the "rebel ruffians" who have forced her "ravin' mad" to seek her husband in the streets. Nora insists that Clitheroe does not fight because he is brave, but because he is a coward afraid to admit that he *is* afraid, just like all the others. Utterly spent, Nora is helped into the apartment by Mrs. Gogan.

Fluther, The Covey, and Peter begin to play a game of chance with some coins. Bessie, who has come out of the tenement, waits until no one is looking and then gives Mollser a glass of milk. As she passes the men, Bessie loudly berates them and the rebels, whose fighting has made it difficult to find food.

The boom of a distant gun is heard; the English have begun using artillery on the streets. Bessie runs back onstage in great excitement. During the bombardment and general confusion, people have broken into the shops and are carrying away all kinds of goods. Bessie has joined the looters and is wearing a new hat and fox fur; she carries three umbrellas under one arm and a box of biscuits under the other. The Covey and Fluther hurry off to join the looters. Bessie and Mrs. Gogan, arguing over which of them will use a neighbor's baby carriage to carry away the loot, also disappear from view.

For a few moments, Peter waits with Mollser for the return of the others. One by one, they return laden with food, boots, clothes—even furniture. Mrs. Gogan and Bessie have joined forces in their looting and are now quite amicable with one another. A shot rings out in the immediate vicinity and everyone bolts into the house.

Brennan comes onstage, supporting Langon, who has been shot in the stomach by English soldiers. Clitheroe follows cautiously with a rifle cocked in his hand. Savagely, Brennan asks Clitheroe why he did not fire to kill the looters. He accuses them of mobbing and attacking the rebel forces. Clitheroe's answer is, "No, no, Bill; bad as they are they're Irish men an' women." Brennan's answer is that they are nothing but "slum lice."

Seeing the men from her window, Nora rushes out of the door and into her husband's arms, begging him to remain with her. Bessie, looking out from her window above, begins to taunt them with their misfortune. Clitheroe responds with tenderness to Nora but insists he must leave with his comrades, who implore him to hurry. Finally, in embarrassment at Nora's refusal to let him go, he pushes her to the ground and stalks off with the others.

Bessie watches Nora for a few moments, then leaves her window, comes out of the tenement, and runs over to the prostrate woman. She picks her up and carries her into the house. Fluther enters, wildly drunk, and is pulled into the house by Bessie.

There is a short pause with no one onstage, and then a long scream of pain is heard from Nora, inside the house. The door opens and Mrs. Gogan and Bessie are seen standing in the hallway. They agree that Nora, whose labor pains have begun, should have a doctor; but Fluther is too drunk to go out, and Mrs. Gogan is afraid to walk the troubled streets. Bessie determines to seek out the doctor herself. She leaves with the prayer that God will "shelter me safely in th' shadow of Thy wings."

A few days elapse between Acts III and IV. The curtain rises on the living room of Bessie's attic apartment. There is a second room, used as a bedroom, offstage. The atmopshere of the room is one of poverty bordering on destitution. The wallpaper is torn and soiled. A shabby dresser stands beside a window draped with the tattered remains of cheap lace curtains. A pane of glass has been shattered by a stray bullet from the fighting outside. Under the window and to the right rests an oak coffin supported by chairs; two flickering candles are nearby. The coffin contains the bodies of Mollser and Nora's premature baby.

In startling contrast to the scene of death are a brass lamp with a fancy shade and a vividly crimson dress, both of them looted. The glare of flames from buildings set afire by the English bombardment is visible through the back window. Now and again the sound of an ambulance can be heard. The residents from the lower floors of the tenement—Peter, The Covey, and Fluther—have gathered in Bessie's attic apartment to escape the gunfire in the streets.

Nora can be heard moaning in the bedroom, deranged by the experiences of the past few days. For three nights, Bessie has been sitting up with her. The men begin to argue about a game of cards they are playing. Bessie appears at the door, telling them to whisper lest they awaken Nora. She sits down in an armchair to rest.

The door opens and Brennan, dressed in civilian clothes, enters. Exhausted and tense, he tells them that Clitheroe was killed at the Imperial Hotel during an English bombardment. The dead man gave him a message just before he died: "Tell Nora to be brave; that I'm ready to meet my God, an' that I'm proud to die for Ireland." Brennan believes Nora's grief will be assuaged by these heroic words, but Bessie assures him he is wrong.

Nora walks in haltingly, clad only in her nightdress. Her manner is strange and distracted. She cries out for her husband and baby and accuses the others of having murdered and hidden them. Bessie persuades Nora to return to the bedroom.

There is the sound of a rifle butt pounding on the door below. Fluther tries to comfort Brennan, urging him to join the card game and, if possible, to control his shaking hands. An English corporal appears to inquire about the "stiff" that must be removed to the cemetery. Mrs. Gogan comes in to accompany her daughter's body to the grave. The Covey, Fluther, Brennan, and Peter carry out the coffin, followed by Mrs. Gogan.

When they return, the corporal informs them that

all the men in the district are to be rounded up and held in a church until the fighting is over. A second English soldier rushes into the room with the news that one of their regiment has been killed by a sniper in the neighborhood. Fluther and the others are forced to leave, guarded by the English soldiers.

Exhausted from the sleepless nights of caring for Nora, Bessie dozes off in the armchair. Nora wanders in and out of the room and sets the table for tea, as if she were expecting her husband. From outside, voices can be heard calling for an ambulance. Nora begins to scream for Clitheroe and the baby. Rushing to the window, she opens it frantically. Soldiers from outside warn her to get away.

With an effort, Bessie pulls Nora from the window but herself staggers against it. Two rifle shots ring out in quick succession. Bessie has been shot by the soldiers who have mistaken her for the rebel sniper. She dies of her wounds, cursing Nora and singing the hymn "I do believe, I will believe that Jesus died for me."

Mrs. Gogan rushes into the room to find out what has happened, sees the dead woman on the floor, and persuades Nora to leave with her. The two English soldiers who had previously been in the house and are the ones responsible for Bessie's death enter agitatedly, expecting to find the sniper. They discover their error, look around the empty room and, noting the table set for tea, decide to have a cup themselves. Outside, the calls for an ambulance continue. There is also the sound of English soldiers singing an army song. As the two soldiers quietly sip their tea, they join their comrades in the chorus:

> Keep the 'owme fires burning
> While your 'earts are yearning;

> Though your lads are far away
> They dream of 'owme. . . .

The English soldiers at tea, Bessie dead on the floor, the fire burning outside—and the final curtain descends on O'Casey's tragedy.

O'Casey used language in *The Plough and the Stars* both to particularize and typify the characters. At the same time, he indicates through these types some of his major themes. The technique is used most effectively in his portrayal of The Figure in the Window. The Figure's words are based on speeches, altered for dramatic effect, of the martyred Padraic Pearse, the young poet and orator whose highly emotional appeals helped spark the Easter Rebellion.

As the scholar W. H. Armstrong pointed out (in *Modern Drama*, Winter 1962), the speeches in Act II are from "The Coming Revolution," "Peace and the Gael," and "At the Grave of O'Donovan Rossa" (a Fenian who, in 1858, was convicted by an English court of treasonable conspiracy and sentenced to life imprisonment).

Comparing The Figure's first speech with the relevant passage in "The Coming Revolution" is instructive, for it suggests that O'Casey not only distilled Pearse's messianic fervor but also refined and emphasized his highly oratorical structure for dramatic reasons. In the following passage from Pearse's speech, the words in italics are those O'Casey puts into the mouth of The Figure:

> I am glad, then that the North has "begun." I am glad that the Orangemen have armed, for *it is a goodly thing to see arms in Irish hands*. I should like to see the A.O.H. armed. I should like to see the Transport Workers armed. I should like to see any and everybody of the Irish citizens armed. We

> must accustom ourselves to the thought of arms, to the sight of arms, to the use of arms. We may make mistakes in the beginning and shoot the wrong people; but *bloodshed is a cleansing and a sanctifying thing, and the nation which regards it as the final horror has lost its manhood. There are many things more horrible than bloodshed; and slavery is one of them.*

Taken out of Pearse's context, the lines are more oracular and more dramatic than in context. Similar ideas about bloodshed as a "cleansing and sanctifying thing" voiced earlier in the speech by Pearse were ignored by O'Casey. Their more tentative and practical character would not as readily evoke what O'Casey had called the "romantic ecstasy" of killing in Langon, Brennan, and Clitheroe.

In The Figure's second speech, O'Casey adapted Pearse's "Peace and the Gael." He added words to Pearse's image of "the red wine of the battlefields," which made more explicit the idea of the redemption of Ireland through an act of human sacrifice. Such changes enabled O'Casey to characterize the Irish rebel as a fanatic militant intent upon self-destruction.

In The Figure's third speech, O'Casey again quoted selectively from Pearse's "Peace and the Gael." He used the words indicated by italics:

> War is a terrible thing, and this is the most terrible of wars. But this war is not more terrible than the evils which it will end or help to end. . . . *War is a terrible thing, but war is not an evil thing.* It is the things that make war necessary that are evil. . . . *Many people in Ireland dread war because they do not know it. Ireland has not known the exhilaration of war for over a hundred years. . . . When war comes to Ireland, she must welcome it as she would welcome the Angel of God.*

O'Casey omitted whatever Pearse said about war as necessary to combat evil and thus emphasized the "exhilaration of war" itself.

Pearse's funeral oration "At the Grave of O'Donovan Rossa" suggested the fourth and last speech of The Figure. By his excisions, O'Casey enhanced Pearse's religious fervor and dogmatism. O'Casey used only those of Pearse's words that are indicated by italics:

> This is a place of peace, sacred to the dead, where men should speak with all charity and with all restraint; but I hold it a Christian thing, as O'Donovan Rossa held it, to hate evil, to hate untruth, to hate oppression, and, hating them, to strive to overthrow them. *Our foes are strong* and wise and wary; *but, strong* and wise and wary *as they are, they cannot undo the miracles of God who ripens in the hearts of young men the seeds sown by the young men of a former generation.* And the seeds sown by the young men of '65 and '67 are coming to their miraculous ripening today. Rulers and Defenders of Realms had need to be wary if they would guard against such processes. Life springs from death; and from the graves of patriot men and women spring living nations. The Defenders of this Realm have worked well in secret and in the open. *They think they have pacified Ireland.* They think that they have purchased half of us and intimidated the other half. *They think* that *they have foreseen everything*; think that they have provided against everything; *but the fools, the fools, the fools!—they have left us our Fenian dead, and while Ireland holds these graves, Ireland unfree shall never be at peace.*

It is after this speech that Brennan, Langon, and Clitheroe exclaim with a kind of vague emotional chauvinism that "Ireland is greater" than "wife" or "mother." One of O'Casey's themes is that the abstract principle of Irish independence is not greater than the moral responsibility a man *should* feel toward his family: many of the rebels were vain, excitable men, incited to spurious heroism by stupid oratory. Despite his disillusionment with Irish militants, O'Casey felt compassion for the "poor, dear dead men" killed in the Easter Rebellion. Clitheroe is not without moments of nobility, and he does die a brave, if deluded, man.

The Plough and the Stars may be viewed as a tragic parable focused on the impoverished Irish working class, but its themes are universal. O'Casey indicated that men make heroic gestures accompanied by grand words but forget their practical and moral responsibilities to the women and children. Even though their bravura speech may amuse or captivate the audience at times, the result can ultimately be tragic in human terms. At the end of Act II, the grandiloquent Clitheroe passionately claims that Ireland means more than a wife; but while he dies for Ireland in a futile rebellion, the crazed Nora causes the death of a compassionate woman who, ironically, is loyal to England and has total contempt for the rebels.

In the sacred name of Ireland, or any other country, waste, destruction, and death shatter the communities of the universal poor—so vulnerable to the course of events over which very often they have no control. Women and children are especially helpless in the force of circumstance. The romantic militants dream of glory and, on occasion, some die for their dreams; but, it is their wives and mothers, often indifferent to the presumably grander issues, who try to sustain human life.

From O'Casey's point of view, those who cared the least for revolutionary principles were those who suffered the most from the Easter Rebellion. He did not feel that it was a truly popular movement (*New York Times*, 12 March 1950):

> If it [the play] has any "significance," it is that a small number—or even one fine mind—may initiate a movement, but cannot bring it to success without the cooperation of what is called "the common people." The gallant men who rose in 1916 to strike for Ireland's independence were defeated; and what they stood for only succeeded when, years later, the people, as a whole, swung round from opposition to support. . . .
>
> Another point is what is called "the looting of goods" in the play. This is usually condemned as a "dastardly insult to the unselfish men who were risking all for Ireland." I don't look at it this way. When they got a chance, they "illegally" seized the brighter goods of life which, with all others, they, too, had the right to have. Here people were usually called "the rats of the slums," but I, who lived among them for so long, knew they had their own intelligence; they had courage, humor and, very often, a great zest for life.

O'Casey's play left scant opportunity for defense of the Easter Rebellion—by the wives of the martyrs, the rebels who survived, or the intellectuals interested in projecting a heroic land of saints and scholars. *The Plough and the Stars* cried out against ignorance that is pernicious, heroism that is spurious, and battle that is futile; it cried out against these evils in the name of the common good.

O'Casey was denounced as a traitor to Ireland for his point of view. Premiered 8 February 1926, at the Abbey Theatre, *The Plough and the Stars* caused riots that seriously hampered performances. The charges against the playwright ranged from negative treat-

ment of the Easter Rebellion to slurs cast upon Irish
womanhood.

Opening night was considered a success by the
Abbey directors although some spectators were visibly
angered and disgusted by the play. Among that group
was Joseph Holloway, the architect who had designed
the Abbey Theatre and was one of its loyal patrons.
He encountered the poet Lyle Donaghy when leaving
the theater. Their conversation—now a classic of theatrical history—has been recorded in Peter Kavanagh's
Story of the Abbey Theatre (1950).

> HOLLOWAY: It is an abominable play.
> DONAGHY: I see nothing abominable in it.
> HOLLOWAY: Then you have a dirty mind.
> DONAGHY: No, I haven't.
> HOLLOWAY: Well you have a filthy mind. There
> are no streetwalkers in Dublin.
> DONAGHY: I was accosted by one only last night.
> HOLLOWAY: There were none in Dublin till the
> Tommies brought them over.

If opening night was a success, it was probably because the deeper implications of the play had not yet
penetrated the minds of many of the audience. On the
following Tuesday and Wednesday after opening
night, a few spectators protested loudly when Brennan, Langon, and Clitheroe carried the flags of the
Irish Volunteers and the Irish Citizen Army into the
bar; they felt it disgraced the memory of those organizations to see their banners in a drinking place. Also,
some spectators were painfully aware of O'Casey's
irony in juxtaposing the drunken brawling in the bar
with The Figure's impassioned plea for war against
the English tyrant.

On Thursday night, rioting broke out among the
audience during the second act. A group led by Mrs.
Sheehy-Skeffington, the widow of a martyr of the

Easter Rebellion, stopped the performance intermittently with shouting, booing, whistle-blowing, and the singing of patriotic songs. The actors managed to continue the performance until the curtain. Early in the third act, however, the play was stopped completely by a barrage of vegetables, shoes, and chairs. A group of men and women clambered on the stage and began a fist-fight with some of the actors.

During this fracas Miss Delany (Nora in the play) was struck in the face by a young man who later denied the blow was intentional. Another rioter attempted to interfere with Barry Fitzgerald (Fluther Good), but he received a blow that sent him crashing back into the audience.

In the midst of the pandemonium, Yeats—eyes flashing, hair flying, hands waving—delivered his famous tirade to the rioting audience (quoted in *Story of the Abbey Theatre*):

> . . . you have disgraced yourselves again. Is this to be an ever-recurring celebration of the arrival of Irish genius? Synge first and then O'Casey. The news of the happenings of the last few minutes will go from country to country. Dublin has once more rocked the cradle of a reputation. From such a scene in this theater went forth the fame of Synge. Equally the fame of O'Casey is born here tonight. This is his apotheosis.

In the days following, the Abbey Theatre received police protection. After an attempt was made to kidnap Barry Fitzgerald, the directors decided it would be better for the actors to remain in the theater between matinée and evening performance.

In her *Journals*, Lady Gregory described O'Casey as being in good spirits during this trying period. At tea with her and Lyle Donaghy, O'Casey related that two

members of the Irish Republican Army assured him
since the riots that they themselves had carried the
Plough and the Stars into pubs. O'Casey seems, however, to have responded more bitterly to the rioting
than Lady Gregory's account would suggest. He had
heard himself scorned for besmirching the virtue of
Irish womanhood, the courage of Irish manhood, and
Ireland itself. He felt himself betrayed by the very
people with whom he had spent years in nationalist
activities.

In November 1927, the Abbey Theatre repertory
company performed *The Plough and the Stars* at the
Hudson Theater in New York. Perhaps the most mean-
ingful comment about the performance was made by
Brooks Atkinson in the *New York Times* (29 November 1927): "After hearing the lines spoken by the Irish
Players, one cannot dissociate this drama from these
actors. They are as natural in their flow of expression
as the eloquence of the dialogue."

In 1934, the Abbey company returned to New York
for an engagement at the Golden Theater. New Yorkers saw *The Plough and the Stars* once again, but it
was the first New York appearance of Barry Fitzgerald
in the role of Fluther Good, which O'Casey had created for him. As usual, he received the highest praise
from the critics. Atkinson wrote that his performance
was such as perhaps no Abbey actor had yet revealed
to a New York audience: "Probably there could be a
funnier actor than Barry Fitzgerald, but probably we
mortals will never see one. His Fluther Good, with his
ignorant piety and general belligerence, is uproarious
comic acting. . . . It is an inspired projection of
groundling character" (*New York Times*, 13 November 1934).

In 1936 film director John Ford adapted *The Plough
and the Stars* into a film version starring Barbara
Stanwyck as Nora Clitheroe and Preston Foster as

Jack Clitheroe. Despite the excellent acting of members of the Abbey Theatre repertory company—Una O'Connor as Mrs. Gogan, Barry Fitzgerald as Fluther Good, J. M. Kerrigan as Peter—Ford's adaptation was a disappointment to all who knew the original play, for it bears only the slightest resemblance to O'Casey's *Plough and the Stars*. Where O'Casey's Jack Clitheroe, for example, dies a heroic if futile death in the fighting of the Easter Rebellion and Nora goes insane, Ford's Jack and Nora walk off into the sunset.

In January 1973, *The Plough and the Stars* was produced at the Vivian Beaumont Theater, Lincoln Center, New York. For the first time in many years, the play had the kind of financial backing it requires for the proper sets. But, as Walter Kerr queried (*New York Times*, 14 January 1973): "Are These O'Casey's Brawling Irish?" The actors did not convey a sense of the strength or thrust of O'Casey's characterizations. And the lack of tension among them caused many in the audience to forget the political tension that was tearing the Irish apart in 1916, a political tension that constitutes an important part of the background of the play. Jack MacGowran, the Irish actor, was the one exception in his role of Fluther Good. (MacGowran, who was an excellent actor and had performed in many of O'Casey's plays, developed the flu during this period and died shortly thereafter.)

Perhaps one day *The Plough and the Stars* will be seen in the United States with all the resources necessary for its production—not only financial backing but a professional cast competent to handle the turbulence of the characters and to convey a sense of Dublin tenement life during the period of the Easter Rebellion. MacGowran's performance showed American audiences just how great that play can be if properly done.

Purple Dust

Published in 1940, *Purple Dust: A Wayward Comedy* was produced in 1945 in Liverpool, England, by the Old Vic Company. The plot develops out of the attempt by two wealthy Englishmen to restore a crumbling Tudor mansion in rural Ireland to its former glory; they also plan to return to nature and to cultivate the old traditions of gentility. According to Mrs. Eileen O'Casey, in her book *Sean* (1972), the symbolic title *Purple Dust* refers to "the wearing to dust of old traditions."

The three acts of the play take place in a room in a decrepit Tudor mansion in Clune na Geera; the time of the play is fixed as "the present," which would be about the time of the outbreak of World War II.

Act I opens on a wide, deep, gloomy room: the floor is laid with black and red flagstones; the walls are timbered with oak beams; the ceiling is formed of the same kind of beams crisscrossing each other. Alternately painted black and white, they give the room the appearance of a gigantic cage.

On the right is a huge, old-fashioned fireplace. Two narrow, arched doorways are at the back, one to the right and the other to the left; between them are two long, deep, mullioned windows. Nearly opposite the fireplace is a wide, arched doorway that leads to the entrance hall. Two antique chairs and a table complete the furnishings.

The First, Second, and Third Workmen are in the room, two with shovels and one with a pickax. The First Workman is described as tall and lean with a foxy face. The Second Workman, O'Dempsey, is also tall with a dreamy look in his eyes; he has a reputation for knowing everything worth knowing about Ireland's legends, myths, and history. The Third Workman is shorter and heavier than the other two.

The First Workman, who has been looking curiously at the huge fireplace, remarks, "Well, of all th' wondhers, to come to live in a house that's half down and it's wanin' over." The workmen discuss the new residents of the mansion until interrupted by their entrance. Cyril Poges, his mistress Souhaun, and the butler Barney dance in through one doorway; Basil Stoke, his mistress Avril, and the maid Cloyne dance in through the other.

They are all similarly attired. Each wears a white smock with a stylized picture of some farm animal; and each carries some dainty little farm implement that looks like a child's toy. Under their smocks, all except Poges and Basil wear the kind of clothing one might expect in the country. Under his smock with its picture of a pig, Poges is dressed in morning clothes, and he wears a top hat. Basil, whose smock has a picture of a hen, is dressed in a typically collegiate jacket, sporty plus fours (a type of baggy knickers), and a cap.

In his stage directions, O'Casey described Cyril Poges, a stockbroker, as sixty-five, not bad looking but inclined to be heavy, with perceptible bags of flesh under his eyes and a protruding stomach. A wealthy, self-made man, Poges is strong willed and fussy. He

always wants his way and is persuaded that whatever
he does is for the best of everyone. Apt to lose his
temper quickly, he shouts at others in the belief that
they must then agree with him. His mistress, Souhaun,
is about thirty-three, a very handsome woman who
describes herself (falsely) as a descendant of the Irish
House of Ormond. Presumably, the Tudor mansion
being renovated is her ancestral home. The butler,
Barney, is a middle-aged Irishman, discontented and
querulous.

In his early thirties, Basil Stoke is tall, thin, languid,
and delicately mannered. He has "a rather gloomy
face which he thinks betokens dignity, made gloomier
still by believing that he is something of a philoso-
pher." Basil's training in philosophy comes from "having passed through Oxford." He claims to descend
from a long line of aristocrats. His money comes from
wise investments made by Poges. Basil's mistress,
Avril, is a pretty, vain girl who cares little about developing her intelligence but relies instead on her
physical charm. The Irish maid, Cloyne, is a good-
looking, stout girl of about twenty-six.

These six meet in the middle of the room and, before the astonished workers, kick their legs about in
what they imagine to be folk dancing. At the same
time, they sing a pastoral song about "man and maid"
who have left the degradation of town life for "the
bosky countrie." After their song is ended, the six
dance out again through the doorways. The 1st Workman comments, "Well, God help the poor omadhauns
[fools]. It's a bad sign to see people actin' like that,
an' they be sober."

The stonemason, O'Killigain, who is in charge of the
repair crew, walks into the room. O'Casey wrote that
he is a tall, fair man with a handsome face. He has had
a pretty tough life, but that has given him confidence
that has been strengthened by wide reading. A Marx-

ist, O'Killigain was wounded during the Spanish Civil
War, in which he fought on the communist side
against the fascists.

Disgusted by Poges's attempts to restore the mansion, O'Killigain observes that "some fool mind will
always see loveliness in rot and ruin." Avril enters
while the men are talking. Although born in Ireland,
she adopts an unnatural attitude of playful condescen-
sion with them, even speaking in an affected brogue.
O'Killigain, with whom she openly flirts, humors her
good-naturedly. They begin a merry little dance while
the others clap and sing. When O'Killigain playfully
slaps her behind, Avril threatens to tell Basil about his
"guttersnipe" behavior. After the Workmen leave,
however, O'Killigain placates her, and they make a
date for the following evening.

Their embrace is interrupted by the entrance of
Souhaun, Poges, Basil, and Cloyne. Poges and Basil
carefully hold framed photographs of themselves,
which they intend to hang on the walls. Avril mentions
that she would like to speak with the Workman said to
be very knowledgeable about Irish history. O'Killigain
cautions her not to make fun of O'Dempsey, "a wan-
dherin' king holdin' th' ages be th' hand."

Enthralled by the thought that the mansion is late
Tudor, Poges tries to recall events and personages he
believes to have existed at the same time. He asks the
name of "the infidel," a follower of "the Prophet," who
was "smashed out of Jerusalem" by the "Lion-hearted
Richard." With complacent confidence, Basil provides
the name of "Genghis Khan," which Poges emphati-
cally accepts as "the name of the bounder."

Poges asks O'Killigain if he too does not feel "the
lovely sensation of—er—er—er—old, unhappy far-off
things, and battles long ago." Obviously impatient,
O'Killigain retorts that life as it is, and will be, moves
him far more. When Poges quotes Wordsworth as say-

ing that too much time is spent thinking about the present and the future, O'Killigain dismisses the poet as "sensitive to everything but man" and a Tory renegade.

Irritated by O'Killigain, Poges peremptorily sends him off to work on the garage, which is to adjoin the mansion. Basil asserts that the Irish are a quaint, charming people if kept under control.

While discussing the need to really understand the country, Poges and Basil get into a heated argument about the nature of the primrose. Basil, who describes himself as a man "versed in all the philosophies of the world," becomes indignant at Poges's calling him a fool. When Poges continues to attack him by pointing out his own accomplishments in the world of finance, Basil is reduced to tears. He goes to his room to recover himself.

Poges turns angrily to his financial newspaper but cannot concentrate on it because of continued interruptions by the First and Third Workmen. They have heard that he is going to start a farm and are eager to sell him "entherprisin' hens," "cocks that'll do you credit," and a cow "with a skin on her as shiny an' soft as the down on a first-class angel's wing." In desperation, he finally shoves them out of the room.

Poges then discovers that the telephone he needs to contact his London broker is not working. He summons O'Dempsey to tell him what is wrong but gets no satisfactory answer. When he snappily calls the workman a fool, trouble begins:

> O'DEMPSEY: Who th' hell are you callin' a fool to?
> . . . Comin' over here an' . . . stickin' their tongue
> out at a race that's oldher than themselves by a
> little like a thousand years, greater in their be-
> ginnin' than they are in their prime; with us
> speakin' with ayse the mighty languages o' the

world when they could barely gurgle a few
sounds, sayin' the rest in the movement of their
fingers.

POGES [*shouting in a rage*]: Go to the devil, man,
and learn manners!

O'DEMPSEY: Hammerin' out handsome golden ornaments for flowin' cloak an' tidy tunic we were,
while you were busy gatherin' dhried grass, an'
dyin' it blue, to hide the consternation of your
middle parts. . . . Fool? It's yourself's the fool,
I'm sayin', settlin' down in a place that's only fit
for the housin' o' dead men! Settlin' here, are
you? Wait till God sends the heavy rain, and the
floods come!

Basil and Avril appear in elegant riding attire, prepared to go horseback riding. Despite O'Killigain's
warning that the horses can be handled only by ac-
complished riders, they leave for their ride. O'Killigain
leaves also.

The disconnected telephone continues to irritate the
already frustrated Poges, who gets into an argument
with Souhaun about whose idea it was in the first
place to settle in the Irish countryside. Exasperated by
his temper, Souhaun (on whom Poges has settled an
income for life) threatens to leave him there alone.

Basil is carried in, bruised and bleeding, by the
Workmen. They found him crawling toward the house
after he had been thrown from his horse. Souhaun asks
about Avril. Speaking figuratively, Basil describes how
"the vixen" cantered away, "naked and unashamed,"
with O'Killigain and left him lying on the ground. The
literal-minded Workmen listen attentively.

Suddenly, plaster falls into the room and a hole appears in the ceiling almost directly over the fireplace.
A bulb attached to a thin rope comes dangling down
through the hole, followed by the face of a workman
named Cornelius. He asks if this is where the light is

to go. Poges screams that he is at the wrong end of the ceiling, and Cornelius disappears back through the hole.

After Souhaun and Poges lead the shaken Basil to his room, the First Workman speaks with mock indignation and delight about the "lassie o' th' house" who went off with O'Killigain, ". . . riding naked through the locality! . . . without as much as a garther on her to keep her modesty from catchin' cold." The Third Workman declares: "This'll denude the disthrict of all its self-denyin' decency." The 1st Workman jumps on a chair and calls excitedly to Cornelius, who thrusts his head through the hole over the fireplace. Told of Avril's naked ride, Cornelius cries out with anguish: "Oh, isn't it like me to be up here outa sight o' th' world, an' great things happenin'!"

Act II takes place in the same gloomy room about 7:30 on a cold, misty morning. Portraits of Basil and Poges are now hanging on the walls. The table is to the left, and two mattresses pushed up against the back wall, next to one another, can be seen. On the mattresses, wrapped up in rugs and blankets, Poges and Basil are twisting about uneasily. The room is without heat, lights, plumbing, and telephone. The hooting of owls is heard, then the faint lowing of cattle, grunting of swine, crowing of cocks, bleating of sheep, and whistling from various directions. Poges sleepily lifts his head, covered by a beret, and awakens Basil.

The two men begin to complain about the present state of affairs: Basil is stiff from his fall, Avril has made a laughing stock of him, neither woman can be controlled because of the life annuities they have settled on them, the workers are demanding higher wages, and the country seems increasingly damp, cold, and noisy. But Poges and Basil decide to make light of their discomforts and try to enjoy every day in the country.

Avril and Souhaun appear, wearing fur coats over their night dresses. Prodded by the two women, the men reluctantly get out of bed. They are both fully dressed with heavy topcoats and scarves. Basil limps off as Cloyne and Barney, also heavily clothed, appear. Poges tries to convince the shivering servants of the benefits of country living. Cloyne leaves to get the Workman who is supposed to be connecting the telephone but returns screaming hysterically that a bull is in the hallway.

In a frenzy of fear, she hangs onto Poges, frustrating his attempts to barricade the doorway with the table and a mattress. Barney rushes off to get Basil to bring his gun. Basil appears with the gun but refuses to get close enough even to see the bull and tries to hand the gun to Poges. "A stylized head, with long curving horns," appears over the barricade thrown up by Poges and lets out a loud bellow. The fleeing Basil throws the gun into the room.

Amidst the wild shouting and spasmodic tugging of Poges and Cloyne, the sound of the First Workman shooing the animal out of the hall can be heard. He reassures the shaking Poges that the animal is, indeed, not a bull but a cow and flatters him on his bravery. Now at his ease, Poges comments solemnly upon Basil, who "ran for his life; think of that. . . . British too, think of that."

Poges asks the First Workman if he is the one who knows all the stories and legends of Ireland, but he is told that it is O'Dempsey he speaks of. With a deferential air toward Poges, the First Workman begins to reminisce about the "grand oul' house . . . when the quality" lived there in ages past. They are enthralled by a vision of silks and satins in sparkling carriages, far removed from the poor, dingy world. The First Workman concludes: "It's meself is sayin' ourselves came late, but soon enough to see the finery fade to purple dust, an' the glow o' the quality turn to murmurin' ashes." Poges swears not to let that beautiful past die out completely.

But Poges has difficulties trying to keep the past alive in the old mansion. Avril and Souhaun, frightened by the sight of huge rats, drop the presumably antique vase and bowl they are carrying. Poges gets furious with the women, who tell him disdainfully that his antique treasures were obvious fakes imported from Singapore. The women leave, reminding Poges that he must move from the doorway a roller he has bought to level the grass.

As Poges stands before the fireplace trying to warm himself, O'Dempsey walks in pushing a wheelbarrow. He asks him to recount something of Irish history. O'Dempsey begins to expound his mythic vision of Irish heroes and English villains, encouraged by O'Killigain, who has entered. Although disconcerted by his slurs on the English nation, Poges is awed by the divinatory manner and rhapsodic tone of O'Dempsey. He asks if others "see" what he envisions. "Barrin' a few an' O'Killigain there," answers O'Dempsey, "they see these things only as a little cloud o' purple dust blown before the wind." Slowly, he walks out.

When Poges tries to defend his countrymen as well as the English Empire, the contemptuous O'Killigain gives the empire a generation or so to exist; and he predicts that it "will be remembered only as a half-forgotten nursery rhyme!" Poges, roaring with rage, says that people who hold such ideas should be jailed.

Souhaun enters and pushes Poges out of the room, insisting he must remove the roller from the doorway. Alone with O'Killigain, Souhaun flirtatiously suggests that with her independent income she could well leave Poges for another man. OKilligain is gallant but uninterested in her offer. They are interrupted by Poges and the 1st Workman, who are pulling a gigantic roller into the room—presumably used to level the lawn, it is large enough to level a hill. Poges insists upon handling it himself. But the moment the First Workman lets go, he loses control of the roller, which is on an inclined passageway, and it smashes through a brick wall offstage. Carried back in a daze, Poges is left alone to recuperate from his accident.

O'Killigain returns and demands that Poges take away the gun Basil is carrying around outside before he hurts someone. Just then a shot is heard. O'Killigain dashes out to see what has happened. A distraught Cornelius pushes his head through the hole in the ceiling and begins to lament the death of the "poor . . . little thing, full o' gaiety an' go!" Poges assumes that Basil has shot poor little Avril for her attentions to O'Killigain. Actually, he has shot the cow under the assumption that it was a wild bull. Cornelius insists upon an indemnity for the dead beast. When Poges finally understands the situation, he says bewilderedly:

> Oh, what a terrible country to have anything to do with! My precious vase is gone, my beautiful bowl is broken; a wall's demolished, and an innocent animal's shot dead: what an awful country to be living in! A no-man's land; a waste land; a wilderness!

At the start of Act III, the sounds of falling rain and high winds are heard; they continue throughout the act, growing louder and faster. Some furniture has now been added to the room. An antique china cabinet is to the right, and on each side of the larger entrance stands an armored figure holding a long halberd. Over them are crossed pennons, green and blue. A blazing fire burns in the fireplace.

Poges hurries over to the telephone, now connected, and finally manages to contact his London stock-broker. He tries to buy shares of a cement company whose prices are "bound to rise" once the Germans begin bombing England, but he learns that the shares are already sold out. Poges cannot believe that there are "so many trying to cash in on splintered bodies."

Canon Creehewel of the local parish comes to visit; he is a man inclined to be overweight and has a hard face. He thanks Poges for past donations and asks his moral support in a campaign against immodest attire and devilish dance halls. He would also like Poges's help in getting rid of O'Killigain, whom he calls "a snake" in their "Garden of Eden." (O'Killigain defended an "immoral" woman from the curate's wrath.)

Immediately after the Canon's invective against women who expose their breasts and legs, Souhaun and Avril walk into the room wearing shorts and halters. They are introduced by the embarrassed Poges as the wives of the household. Poges makes another donation, happily accepted by the Canon. Remarking that the soft rainfall may change into a downpour and he has a long way to go, the Canon leaves.

Despite Basil's protests, Avril insists on leaving by herself. Both men suspect she has gone off to meet O'Killigain and they leave. Souhaun calls in O'Dempsey and asks if he knows where O'Killigain has gone. She learns from him that he and Avril are together. Souhaun is upset. After a pause, O'Dempsey predicts that one day soon Souhaun, whom he calls "hand-some" and "sensible," will dance away from the brag-gart Poges, "who thinks the world spins round on th' rim of a coin." He suggests that Souhaun would be happy with him. Although touched by his proposal, Souhaun turns and slowly walks out of the room.

When Poges returns, the Workmen try to move a huge quattrocento bureau into the room through an arched doorway obviously too small to permit its ingress. Under Poges's hysterical orders, they finally force it into the room, but not until the columns of the doorway are snapped off and the bureau itself badly damaged. Poges is in a rage with everyone. His rantings about the damage to the priceless "quattrocento" are accompanied by peals of thunder that become louder and louder.

Souhaun, Basil, and the two servants enter. When O'Dempsey talks back to Poges and Basil in a way they consider an impertinence to his "betters," all three begin to argue about whose family line is the oldest. Soon they are fighting about the historic primacy of Celts compared to Anglo-Saxons. O'Killigain, who has also entered the room, joins O'Dempsey in denouncing the "upstart" English.

Another loud peal of thunder is heard, and the room darkens a little. O'Killigain dismisses the Workmen, saying that it is a waste of time to try to buttress up the decrepit mansion, particularly with the heavy rains coming. O'Dempsey and O'Killigain urge Souhaun and Avril to leave their English providers, to go with them into the enchanted hills where love "can fix or flutther th' stars o' th' sky an' change th' shining moon into a lamp for two," and to live a truly free, joyous life. O'Dempsey promises to return on horseback for Souhaun; O'Killigain will come for Avril in a boat once the expected floods have arrived. They leave to the jeering insults of Poges and Basil, who cannot believe their mistresses will take such offers seriously.

The village Postmaster, who is also in charge of the telephone system, comes in to inform Poges that he is not to use the service after ten at night. While the two men argue with one another—the room has darkened still more—a horse can be heard in the distance, galloping away.

The Figure of a man suddenly appears at the entrance to the hall. He is dressed in black oilskins, a hood over his head and a blue mask on his face; the mask is illuminated by rays of flickering lightning. The Figure looks like "the spirit of the turbulent waters of the rising river." He speaks in a deep voice as the room darkens and the wind rises:

> The river has broken her banks and is rising high; . . . Trees of an ancient heritage . . . are torn from the power of the place they were born in. . . . Those who have lifted their eyes unto the hills are firm . . . in the hills is safety; but a trembling perch in the highest place on the highest house shall be the portion of those who dwell in the valleys below!

Frightened by his words, Cloyne and Barney rush up to the roof for safety. Poges calls out for Souhaun, but Avril, appearing with a suitcase in her hand, tells him that she left with O'Dempsey (on the galloping horse heard earlier). She herself runs to O'Killigain, who appears dripping wet in the doorway. Basil and Poges sneer that Avril, who carries off the "booty" she has gathered, will make O'Killigain happier with her "harlot's fortune." Good-humoredly, he replies that of course he will be happier: "You have had your day, like every dog. Your Tudors have had their day, and they are gone; and th' little heap o' purple dust they left behind them will vanish away in th' flow of the river." After they leave, O'Killigain is heard singing.

Poges listens until Basil clutches his arm, screaming that the waters are tumbling toward them. Basil tears up the passageway to the roof, followed by Poges, who laments:

> My poor little quattrocento, the waters are about to cover thee! My comfort's gone, and my house

of pride is straining towards a fall. Would to God
I were in England, now that winter's here!

The final curtain descends.

In a letter to his dear friend, the critic George Jean
Nathan, O'Casey discussed the genesis of *Purple Dust*
(quoted in volume 1 of D. Krause's *Letters of Sean
O'Casey*, 1975):

> I think it is, in some ways, an odd play. . . . At
> first it was to be just a skit on the country; but it
> changed a little into, maybe, a kind of an allegori-
> cal form. The idea crept into my head after a visit
> to a family living in a Tudor House here; suffering
> all kinds of inconveniences because of its age &
> history; going about with lantern, & eating in semi-
> gloom. Terrible torture for the sake of a tumble-
> down house with a name! I've never gone there
> since. I was perished with the cold, & damaged
> with the gloom.

In his "odd" play *Purple Dust*, O'Casey created several types of character, most notably, the English landlords Cyril Poges and Basil Stoke, and the Irish
workers—the First Workman, O'Killigain, and
O'Dempsey.

The choleric Poges screams, yells, rants, and raves at
everyone who does not follow his orders immediately,
agree with his opinions, or express a sense of the peace
and good will he insists is to be found in the country.
When Basil, who "has passed through Oxford," questions his educational background in philosophical matters, Poges answers with contempt:

> I was reared any old how; and here I am today, a
> money'd man, able to say to almost any man,
> come, and he cometh, and to almost any other
> man, go, and he goeth—and quick too; . . . with-

> out an inherited penny to help! . . . And that's
> more than some of them can say. And I never
> passed through Oxford!

Despite his ability to make money, Poges is an ignorant man who knows nothing of literature, history,
or antique furnishings. (His notion of the proper way
to restore the Tudor mansion is to paint its rotting
beams in bright colors.) Although Poges professes a
desire to return to the simplicity and beauty of nature,
he is more concerned about building a garage and
fixing the telephone than in learning the difference
between a cow and a bull, or in knowing when the
floods common to the area will inundate the mansion.
Even in the country, he wears morning clothes and a
tall hat.

But Poges, for all of his deficiencies, is a man of will.
The melancholic Basil, on the other hand, is a total
incompetent—unenterprising, sentimental, and affected. He relies upon family name, having "passed
through Oxford," and Poges's financial wisdom to get
him through life. His arrogance combined with stupidity make him an insufferable pedant, illustrated in the
outré jargon he uses to anatomize the primrose for the
sake of elucidating the minds of the others:

> If we take the primrose, however, into our syn-
> thetical consideration, as a whole, or, *a priori*, as a
> part, with the rest of the whole of natural objects
> or phenomena, then there is, or may be, or can be
> a possibility of thinking of the flower as of above
> the status, or substance, or quality of a fragment;
> and, consequently, correlating it with the whole,
> so that, to a rational thinker, or logical mind, the
> simple primrose is, or may become, what we may
> venture to call a universal. See?

Basil is as insensitive to the country as his compatriot. He, too, dresses in inappropriate attire—plus fours or an elegant riding habit.

Poges and Basil are essentially comic types, almost caricatures. The Irish characters, although often funny, tend to be more complex as types: the First Workman, a foxy sycophant; O'Killigain, a realist; and O'Dempsey, a romantic.

Although the First Workman is the first to mention the absurdity of trying to restore the mansion, he slyly and cunningly caters to Poges's fantasies, probably in the hope of selling his "entherprisin' hins" at a good price. But, he does seem to fall in genuinely with Poges's melancholy contemplation of a lost gentility: it is the First Workman who bemoans the fact that "we" have lived to see "the finery fade to purple dust."

O'Killigain is a realist cast in the mold of the proletarian hero: a militant Marxist, intelligent, well-read, and virile, with a sincere love for nature and art, as well as womanhood. Although O'Killigain is Irish, he has a sense of mission toward the common man that is universal in scope. He denigrates the "fool mind" that sees "loveliness in rot and ruin"; he dismisses Wordsworth as a Tory renegade "sensitive to everything but man"; and he denounces the British Empire, which "will be remembered only as a half-forgotten nursery rhyme." At the end of the play, the eminently practical O'Killigain admits that he will enjoy the money carried away by Avril from her former lover. He tells the sneering Englishmen that they have had their day, like the Tudors before them, who are now gone—and "th' little heap o' purple dust they left behind" will not survive the flood.

Although the realist O'Killigain has many values, principles, and ideals in common with his friend, whom he describes as "a wanderin' king holdin' the ages be th' hand," O'Dempsey is essentially a dreamy-eyed romantic and a visionary. O'Dempsey envisions a supernatural link between mythical and historical Irish figures and such men as himself and O'Killigain. He also weaves into his vision a kind of nature mysticism:

> I hear sthrange things be day, an' see sthrange things be night when I'm touched be the feel of the touch of the long-handed Lugh. . . . Then every rib o' grass grows into a burnished fighter that throws a spear, or waves a sword, an' flings a shield before him. Then Ireland crinkles into a camp, an' kings an' sages, queens an' heroes, saints an' harpers stare me in the face, an' bow, an' pass, an' cry out blessing an' vict'ry too, for Heber's children, with the branch of greatness waving in their hands!

In Irish mythology, "the long-handed Lugh" is known as the sun god, god of light, and god of genius, who gave the various arts to the native Irish. "Heber's children" (of whom O'Dempsey is one) has reference to the descendants of one of the kings of ancient Ireland.

When O'Dempsey recites the Irish past in this rapt, almost incantatory manner—as he did to the awed Poges—he is fulfilling a role comparable to that of the Gaelic *Fili* thought to live in pre-Christian Ireland. The *Fili*, who often wrote compositions in honor of the heroic achievements of men, was considered a poet, scholar, historian, and judge. He was also thought to have the supernatural powers of a prophet and seer.

But O'Dempsey's prophetic warning that the heavy rains and the floods are coming to destroy the mansion are dismissed by Poges as the words of a fool. O'Dempsey realizes that for most people, including his own countrymen, the heroic figures of the past are only "a little cloud o' purple dust blown before the wind."

The symbolic title *Purple Dust*—"the wearing to dust of old traditions"—indicates various themes that develop out of the dramatic action. When Avril deserts Basil for O'Killigain, and Souhaun, Poges for O'Dempsey, it is more than true love defeating a monied arrangement. Symbolically, it is the triumph of the Irish over the English, of true aristocracy over specious gentility, of self-determination over imperialism, of sensuousness over puritanism, of nature over pastoral affectation, of knowledge over pedantry, of communism over capitalism. It is the ideal espoused by James Larkin, leader of the Irish Transport and Workers' Union, of "the flower *and* the loaf" for the common man.

When O'Casey introduced the Figure of the man at the end of Act III, he changed his "odd" play into "a kind of allegorical form" whereby events, characters, and settings convey a theme beyond the specific dramatic action. The Figure, which symbolizes the rising river, also symbolizes the river of Time. Its inevitable flood will destroy the Tudor house, which represents for the present age social humbug, stuffy convention, and political and religious cant.

The theatrical history of *Purple Dust* is unusual even for an O'Casey play: it involves misappropriation, national antipathies, and, possibly, political prejudice. In the last volume of his autobiography, *Sunset and Evening Star*, O'Casey wrote that (about 1940) the critic George Jean Nathan, a personal friend, had promised to bring about an American production of the play. While waiting for Nathan to write him, O'Casey received an unsigned letter from the London Theatre Club, asking an option to produce the play.

He immediately responded, refusing permission because of the expected American production.

O'Casey then received a second letter from the producer connected with the theater club, announcing that the play was already in rehearsal; the producer asked that O'Casey give his formal permission. O'Casey's written reply was an emphatic "no." A third letter came announcing that James Agate, a famous critic generally unsympathetic to O'Casey's work, had been invited to review the play for the coming issue of the Sunday *London Times*. O'Casey was incensed but could not prevent the production or review. (Apparently no legal means of redress were available to him.) Agate denounced *Purple Dust* as a worthless drama and a vicious attack on England at a time when, owing to the German bombings, she was distracted, hopeless, and unable to reply.

Nathan never was able to get an American production because many backers felt it would be unwise to produce a play seemingly critical of England, a wartime ally.

In 1945, the play was produced in Liverpool, England, by the Old Vic Company—with O'Casey's permission. Although the production went well, it was not notable, and O'Casey still longed for the American production that Nathan had failed to arrange despite his efforts. O'Casey had come to feel that audiences in the United States were more sympathetic to his work than those in London; and he could rely on making some badly needed money, particularly in New York, should there be a production of the play.

But it was not until 1957, some eighteen years after it was written, that *Purple Dust* was finally produced in the United States, at the Off-Broadway Cherry Lane Theater in New York. Paul Shyre was one of the producers; he also played the role of Basil Stoke. Philip Burton directed the performance, and Lester Polakov, who was acclaimed by all the critics for his ingenuity, designed the settings. The production received good reviews for the most part.

Purple Dust was not seen again in London until 1962, when it was produced as one of several plays in an O'Casey Festival, celebrated at the Mermaid Theatre in London. The reviewers were no more enthusiastic about the play than James Agate had been several years before, during World War II. Both the *London Times* drama critic (19 August 1962) and Kenneth Tynan of the *Observer* (19 August 1962) judged it an "inferior" work.

O'Casey was so disgusted by what he considered their ignorance that he replied in a scathing article called "Purple Dust in Their Eyes" (published in *Under a Colored Cap*, 1963). He began by taking issue with the remark of the *London Times* critic that a dramatist who likes people yet believes in revolution is in an uncomfortable position. Poges and Basil, according to this critic, are likeable characters "in whom eccentricities are so delightful." O'Casey insisted he was not at all "uncomfortable" as a revolutionist, for the revolution envisioned in *Purple Dust*, rather than being violent, is one "brought about by Time and the slow-moving or swift-moving winds of change." Though Poges and Basil may be likeable, if not exactly lovable, Time and Change "don't give a damn." These "eccentrics" so loved by the *London Times* critic, says O'Casey, "are always a nuisance, sometimes an actual menace, to those who live with them, so that if Time and Change go too slowly, Life itself may shove them out of the way."

O'Casey's reply to the *London Times* critic was determined but dispassionate in tone. To Tynan's criticism, it was one of dislike and contempt. Tynan had dismissed *Purple Dust* as a "tenuous one-joke jape." O'Casey found the judgment disappointing in view of the amount of time he had spent in its creation. He admitted, however, that time, labor, and thought will not in and of themselves make a play worthy: history must decide.

But he described certain of Tynan's observations as "blimpish." Tynan identified Poges and Basil with the English upper class, which (contrary to O'Casey's representation) knows a great deal about country life, according to Tynan. O'Casey countered that the two characters are businessmen, not members of the upper class: they are essentially plutocrats—Basil pretends to be a scholar—who only ape the upper classes.

O'Casey also took issue with Tynan's wry dismissal of Ireland's past glories "as four-fifths incomprehensible" to the normal audience. The Sword of Light, a symbol from Celtic mythology, is, as O'Casey pointed out, universal and appears in many different literary works, for example, the Excalibur of Arthurian legend. O'Casey accused Tynan of dismissing the play primarily because it "laughs and makes merry."

There has been no other noteworthy production of *Purple Dust* in America since the one at the Cherry Lane Theater in 1957. It is a pity, for the play, like all of O'Casey's works, is eminently theatrical—lyrical and philosophical, serious and comic, all at the same time.

Red Roses for Me

Red Roses for Me, a play in four acts, was published in 1942; it was produced at the Olympia Theatre, in Dublin, on 15 March 1943. The play is about a young railroad switchman, Ayamonn Breydon, who is a leader of the Dublin transport workers' strike of 1913–14, during which he loses his life. The title of the play comes from an old Dublin ballad, "She Carries a Bunch of Red Roses for Me," which is introduced in the first act and serves as a theme song for the play:

A sober black shawl hides her body entirely,
Touch'd by th' sun and th' salt spray of the sea;
But down in th' darkness a slim hand, so lovely,
Carries a rich bunch of red roses for me.

Her petticoat's simple, her feet are but bare,
An' all that she has is but neat an' scantie;
But stars in th' deeps of her eyes are exclaiming
I carry a rich bunch of red roses for thee!

No arrogant gem sits enthron'd on her forehead,
Or swings from a white ear for all men to see;
But jewel'd desire in a bosom most pearly,
Carries a rich bunch of red roses for me!

The action of the play covers several days before Easter, just preceding the strike. Acts I and II are set in the home of Ayamonn Breydon and his mother; Act III, in a street beside a bridge over the Liffey River; and Act IV, on the grounds of the Protestant church St. Burnupus.

The curtain opens on the front room of a two-room apartment located in a poor working-class district. The whitewashed walls are fading into a rusty yellowish tinge. A fireplace with a brightly burning fire is on the right. On the left, toward the back, is a door that leads to an offstage bedroom.

At the back, toward the right, is the main door, which leads to the outside hall. To the left of the main door is a basket partially filled with actors' costumes. Above the basket are two pictures hanging on the wall: one is a small, inexpensive reproduction of *The Cornfield*, by John Constable, an English painter of the late eighteenth–early nineteenth centuries; the other, a childlike pastel of angels blowing a curved, golden trumpet, is in the manner of Fra Angelico, an Italian painter of the early fifteenth century. To the right of the main door is a kitchen dresser, the upper shelf of which is filled with a row of worn-looking books.

Also at the back is a large window, through which is visible the top of a railway signal with green and red lights on its transverse arms. Under the window, a geranium, a musk, and a fuchsia plant grow in biscuit tins placed on a bench. Next to the window is a horsehair sofa with folded bedding, which indicates its use as a bed at night. On an old chair in the center of the room are a smoky oil lamp, some books, drawing paper, colored chalks, pen, and ink.

It is early evening, and a spring rain is falling heavily. Ayamonn, tall, well-built, with deep brown eyes and fair hair, is standing near his mother, who is seated. She is about fifty years of age; her face is marked with struggle and hard work. Over shabby but clean clothes, each wears a brilliantly colored costume: Mrs. Breydon's is a rich-blue velvet cloak, embroidered with silver lace; Ayamonn's is a bright-green silken doublet covered with a crimson velvet, sleeveless cloak edged with white fur. The back part of the cloak is padded to form a hump between his shoulders.

Mother and son have their heads cocked, as if listening to something. We learn from their whispers that knocking at the hall door has interrupted their rehearsal of a scene from Shakespeare's *Henry VI: Part III*. They purposely did not answer, and the caller has gone away. Ayamonn continues to recite lines from the scene in which the crippled Gloucester assassinates the king.

Again they are interrupted by a knock to which they do not respond. When it is quiet outside, Ayamonn tells his mother of his plans for staging the scene they are rehearsing. He wants to borrow a chair with arms, which he will paint a golden color; for the back of the chair, he will paint on thin cardboard "a cunning design of the House of Lancaster, the red rose, so that it'll look like a kingly seat." (This is the first of several allusions made to "the red rose.") The assassination scene is to be presented for the benefit of the transport workers' union, to which Ayamonn belongs. There will also be a minstrel show on the program, for which he has written the song "Red Roses for Me."

Mrs. Breydon is worried about her son's health. She cautions him against trying to do too much—"sketchin', readin', makin' songs, an' learning Shakespeare." With only a few hours of sleep, he must soon leave for a full night's work in the railway yards. But Ayamonn insists that his very life needs all of these artistic and intellectual pursuits. Mrs. Breydon is also concerned about rumors that the union may go on strike for a wage increase of a shilling a week, but Ayamonn is sure that the company will grant the workers their meager demand.

Hesitantly, Mrs. Breydon turns to the subject of Sheila Moorneen, Ayamonn's sweetheart. Although liking the girl, she fears that religious and class differences between them bode no good for the future. The Breydons are poor, working-class Protestants; Sheila, a strict Roman Catholic, is the daughter of a sergeant in the Royal Irish Constabulary, a police force traditionally the enemy of the workers.

Impatiently, Ayamonn dismisses all of his mother's worries. Although she was of tremendous importance and help in his childhood, he feels that they are now drifting apart in their ideas of what is important. Ayamonn mentions that he is expecting a visit that evening from his friend Mullcanny, who has promised to loan him a scientific book called *The Riddle of the Universe*. Mrs. Breydon believes that the neighbors are becoming increasingly hostile toward Mullcanny, an atheist, because of his open mockery of their sacred beliefs.

Mrs. Breydon, who has put on her shawl, begins to move quietly toward the door when it suddenly opens. Several neighbors are standing in the hallway, among them Eeada, Dympna, and Finnoola. In his stage directions, O'Casey wrote: "All their faces are stiff and mask-like, holding tight an expression of dumb resignation; and are traversed with seams of poverty and a hard life."

Dympna is carrying a statue of the Virgin Mary, which usually stands in a small niche directly across from the door of the Breydon apartment. The statue, with a crown castellated like the towers of Dublin, is faded and soiled. In order to wash it, the neighbors have come to request a packet of soap, which Mrs. Breydon willingly contributes. As they leave, Mrs.

Breydon starts to follow them until noticed by her son. He does not want her to go out on such a cold, rainy night, but she insists that a sick neighbor needs her attention.

As Mrs. Breydon opens the door to leave, Sheila, Ayamonn's girlfriend, enters. She is an attractive, fairly tall girl of about twenty-three with a graceful carriage. Her large brown eyes, as described by O'Casey, are "sympathetic" but "dim, now and again, with a cloud of timidity." Eager to be alone with Sheila, Ayamonn now encourages his mother to visit her sick friend.

After Mrs. Breydon leaves, Sheila tells Ayamonn that she is angry at him for having failed to answer her earlier knock. Apologetic, he explains that he was rehearsing his part for the union show and did not realize it was she. Sheila complains that he treads so many paths in life, it is impossible for them to plan a future together. Ayamonn does not agree:

> I tell you life is not one thing, but many things, a wide branching flame, grand and good to see and feel, dazzling to the eye. . . . I am not one to carry fear about with me as a priest carries the Host. Let the timid tiptoe through the way where the paler blossoms grow; my feet shall be where the redder roses grow, though they bear long thorns, sharp and piercing, thick among them.

When he sees that Sheila softens a bit, Ayamonn tries to embrace her and calls her "a bonnie rose, delectable and red."

They are disturbed by the appearance of Brennan o' the Moore, an old man with a bald head and long white beard, who walks in complaining that no one responded to his earlier knock. A Protestant like the Breydons, Brennan is a wealthy slumlord, constantly anxious about the fate of the Bank of Ireland, which serves as depository for what he calls his "few pennies."

Brennan, who carries a melodeon on his back, has just finished composing lyrics for the song Ayamonn wrote for the minstrel show. A young worker called Sam waits outside to sing it for Ayamonn's approval. Delighted, Ayamonn urges Brennan to get the singer immediately. Sheila insists that they speak privately, for she must soon leave, but Ayamonn pleads that she remain at least long enough to hear the song. Brennan returns with Sam, whose "face is pale and mask-like in its expression of resignation to the world and all around him."

Roory O'Balcaun, "a zealous Irish Irelander," enters with some magazines he has brought for his friend Ayamonn. A stout, middle-aged man, Roory is dressed in homespun coat, cap, and knee breeches covered by a trench coat (typically worn by Irish rebels). Although himself a worker, Roory objects to the use of a "foreign" minstrel show to raise funds for the union.

To the accompaniment of Brennan's melodeon, Sam sings the first verse of the song. He is interrupted by the appearance of Mullcanny, a lusty, restless young man dressed in ill-fitting tweeds (fairly typical of the civil servant). Sam finishes the song—obviously written in honor of Sheila—but she stalks out of the room, remarking to Ayamonn as she goes that he will probably never see her again.

The door is suddenly flung open after her exit, and the neighbors who had earlier come with the statue almost tumble into the room. Eeada wails that the Virgin Mary has disappeared from its customary niche in the wall. Ayamonn reassures his neighbors that he himself will look for the missing statue. Mullcanny accuses the neighbors of wasting their time looking for gods made in "their own ignorant images" and leaves. Roory—himself a Catholic—predicts trouble for Mull-

canny, but Ayamonn insists that no harm is meant by
the freethinker.

When Roory asks "what kid" sketched the angels in
the picture on the wall, Ayamonn answers that he did.
Roory cannot understand why anyone would have interest in art or literature not specifically Irish. He believes that only the Irish rebels have "th' light" (an
allusion to the Sword of Light common in Celtic folk-
lore that came to symbolize the Fenian "light of freedom"). Although Ayamonn does not agree with
Roory's total absorption in Ireland to the exclusion of
all else, the act ends with the two men clasping hands
and singing a verse from a revolutionary song.

Act II takes place the next night; the setting is the
same as in the previous act. The rain has stopped, and
the moon is shining through the back window of the
apartment. Counting some pennies, Ayamonn tells his
mother that he hopes to buy another Constable reproduction with the extra shilling the union is expecting
to win. Brennan enters carrying a package that contains the missing statue of the Virgin. He has had it
repainted for the sake of a child in the building who
loves it: ". . . the lost image [is] transfigured . . . the
white dress is spotless, the blue robe radiant, and the
gold along its border and on the crown is gleaming."
Ayamonn, who is annoyed with Brennan for having
taken the statue, orders him to replace it in the niche
immediately.

Mrs. Breydon leaves for the funeral of the neighbor
she visited the previous night. Ayamonn tries to recite
his lines from *Henry VI*, but he is intermittently prevented from doing so by the comments of Brennan,
now returned from having replaced the statue. Roory
comes in and reports that Mullcanny is on his way to
the apartment with the book for Ayamonn. Roory, sec-
onded by Brennan, strongly condemns Mullcanny for
his atheism, but Ayamonn says that he will defend any

honest man who seeks the truth, "though his way isn't my way."

Roory and Brennan begin a fierce argument about the validity of their respective faiths, Catholicism and Protestantism, during which Mullcanny walks in. He listens for a few seconds and then ridicules both disputants for believing in "the coloured slime of the fairy-tales that go to make what is called religion." He gives Ayamonn the promised book, which, he says, will give a true and scientific history of man's evolution from an animal state. Pointing out a drawing in the book to Ayamonn, Mullcanny tells him to note the "human form unborn. The tail—look; the os coccyges [plural of coccyx] sticking out a mile." After Mullcanny's departure, Brennan says the book should be banned and Roory says he would like to see the atheist clapped in jail for his beliefs. Sadly, Ayamonn asks Roory if that is "th' sort o' freedom you'd bring to Ireland . . . ?"

The voice of Sheila, calling to Ayamonn, is heard outside the door. Quickly, he hurries the two men into the room offstage so that he can speak to her privately and opens the door. Sheila wants Ayamonn to forget his intellectual and artistic interests and to stop consorting with people (like Mullcanny) who can harm him. She asks that he concentrate instead on earning a better living so that they can marry in the near future. Sheila says that she would look comical in the "scantie petticoat," "sober black shawl," and "bare feet" described by Ayamonn in his song. His answer is that with "red roses in your hand, you'd look beautiful."

Outside in the street a fight can be heard, but Ayamonn dismisses it as some drunken row. Sheila warns him not to participate in the forthcoming strike. She has been told that if Ayamonn separates himself from the men and sticks to his job, he will soon become a foreman. (Her information comes from In-

spector Finglas, a member of the police, who loves
Sheila although he is a Protestant.) If Ayamonn is
promoted to foreman, continues Sheila, they can soon
marry. Horrified by her request that he desert his fellow workers purely for self-interest, Ayamonn repulses
Sheila when she tries to propitiate him.

Mullcanny hurries into the room, pale, frightened,
his clothes disordered and blood on his face. He has
been assaulted by a mob of angry believers. A stone
crashes through the window. Its sound brings Brennan
and Roory in from the room offstage to see what has
happened. Immediately, a second stone comes crashing through the window. Brennan throws himself flat
on the floor, Mullcanny fearfully crouches down, and
Roory falls to his hands and knees, "keeping his head
as low as possible, so that he resembles a Moham-
medan at his devotions." Sheila huddles into a corner.

Grabbing a stick, the angry Ayamonn rushes outside
to disperse the mob pursuing Mullcanny. From their
various squatting postures on the floor, the men begin
to argue with one another:

> ROORY: This is what you bring down on innocent
> people with your obstinate association of man
> with th' lower animals.
> MULLCANNY: Only created impudence it is that
> strives to set yourselves above the ape's forma-
> tion, genetically present in every person's body.
> BRENNAN: String out life to where it started, an'
> you'll find no sign, let alone a proof, of the dig-
> nity, wisdom, an' civility of man ever having
> been associated with th' manners of a monkey.

Ayamonn and his mother walk in together; they are
surprised to find the angry men squatting on the floor.
Embarrassed, the men get up. Anxiously Mrs. Breydon
looks at her plants, fearful that they have been dam-

aged by the stones crashing through the window over them.

The neighbors appear in the open doorway, "their pale faces still wearing the frozen look of resignation." Softly, they sing to the newly painted statue, which they believe has returned by miracle to its niche in the wall:

> Oh! Queen of Eblana's poor children,
> Bear swiftly our woe away;
> An' give us a chance to live lightly
> An hour of our life's dark day!
> Lift up th' poor heads ever bending,
> An' light a lone star in th' sky,
> To show thro' th' darkness, descending,
> A cheerier way to die.

The neighbors leave, followed by Mullcanny, Brennan, and Roory. After Mrs. Breydon goes to her room, Ayamonn curtly asks Sheila to leave also. The Rector of the Breydons' church, Reverend Clinton, enters the room and greets Ayamonn warmly. As they speak, two railway men, whose faces "stonily stare in front of them," come in with the news that the strike will definitely take place despite the government's determination to prevent it.

Sheila begs the Rector to stop Ayamonn from participating in the strike lest he come to harm, but he feels he has no right to do so. As the curtain descends, Sheila weeps quietly and the neighbors in the hall outside intone the hymn to the Virgin Mary.

Act III, a poetic fantasy that does not further the plot action, will be discussed later in the chapter.

Act IV takes place in part of the grounds surrounding the Protestant church St. Burnupus, located in a poor district. The grounds are planted with a rowan tree, shrubs, and flowers. An iron railing, almost hidden by a green and golden hedge, runs along the back.

In the center is a wide gate that gives admittance to the grounds. To the right is the porch of the church; the wall and entrance are visible.

It is a warm evening, the vigil of Easter, and the Rector is sitting at a table on the grounds, looking at what are probably his sermon notes. Samuel, the caretaker, tells him that the vestrymen Foster and Dowzard consider the flowers decorating the church for the Easter service a popish emblem. Samuel says that Foster "near went daft" when he saw the cross of daffodils made by Ayamonn for the altar. But the Rector refuses to remove the flowers or the cross.

Mrs. Breydon, followed by Sheila, enters. Both women ask the Rector's help in persuading Ayamonn to stay out of the strike, but again the Rector tells them that he does not have the authority or the knowledge to advise him. To the left, on a path outside the back hedge, Inspector Finglas appears in full uniform; to the right, Ayamonn appears, followed by several workers, among them the tenement neighbors from the previous acts. As O'Casey described them, "they hold themselves erect now; their faces are still pale, but are set with seams of resolution. Each is wearing in the bosom a golden-rayed sun." Brennan, who was part of the group, comes in and sits down on the porch steps.

The Inspector demeans Ayamonn for defying the law, for "only a shilling" at that. Ayamonn retorts:

> A shilling's little to you, and less to many; to us it is our Shechinah [Shekinah], showing us God's light is near; showing us the way in which our feet must go; a sun-ray on our face; the first step taken in the march of a thousand miles.

When the Inspector warns that the strikers will learn a lesson that day, Mrs. Breydon denounces him for his arrogance. She blesses her son in his venture and hopes that the strike will add "another inch to the world's welfare." After the Inspector departs, Ayamonn leaves with his followers.

The Rector invites Mrs. Breydon and Sheila into the church for tea. A distant booing accompanied by the rattling of stones is heard. The conservative vestrymen Dowzard and Foster dash into the church grounds. Dressed in the uniforms of railway foremen, they have been attacked by the strikers for scabbing. In a rage, they predict that the "popish" workers—led by Ayamonn—will soon begin to massacre all Protestants. When the Rector comes out of the church, Foster demands that he excommunicate Ayamonn for defying the law, but the Rector refuses even to consider the idea. Meanwhile, Samuel has surreptitiously passed the cross of daffodils taken from the altar over to Dowzard.

In the distance, a bugle call sounds the charge of the police against the strikers. Foster and Dowzard begin to stamp on the cross of daffodils until the sight of fleeing men and women sends them rushing onto the church porch. Obviously in great pain, the tenement neighbor Finnoola comes slowly along the path outside the hedge and sinks down next to the central gateway. She brings a message from Ayamonn, who has been killed by a bullet through the chest: "He whispered it in me ear. . . . He said this day's but a day's work done, an' it'll be begun again tomorrow." Ayamonn also requested that the Rector permit his body to lie in the church that night and that he look after his mother in the future.

The curtain descends briefly to indicate the passing of time.

A crowd has gathered outside the church to wait for Ayamonn's body. Holding a bunch of crimson roses in her hand, Sheila waits under the rowan tree. Partly behind it, the Inspector stands alone. Mrs. Breydon is near the gateway. Foster and Dowzard are on the steps of the porch. In front of them is the Rector, a surplice over his cassock.

A bier, bearing the draped body of Ayamonn, is carried into the grounds by the workers, among whom is Brennan. When the bier passes near her, Sheila lays the bunch of crimson roses on the body's breast. Foster and Dowzard demand that the Rector refuse to allow the body to be carried into the church, but he dismisses them with contempt. The cortege and Mrs. Breydon enter the church for the funeral service.

Some of the workers, Sheila, the Inspector, and Brennan remain outside. One of the workers remarks that Ayamonn "died for us," and another adds, "It was a noble an' a mighty death." The Inspector comments that it was hardly noble to die for a shilling, but Sheila says that maybe Ayamonn "saw the shilling in th' shape of a new world." When the Inspector tries to comfort her, Sheila recalls Ayamonn's having said that "roses red were never meant for me." Suddenly, she turns on the Inspector, calling him a killer, and runs out of the gate.

Mrs. Breydon comes from the church, accompanied by the Rector; she reflects sadly that the body of her son must now lie in the darkened church until the burial. To comfort her, the Rector orders Samuel to turn up the lights. After they leave, Brennan bribes Samuel into opening the church door so that he can say a final good-by to his friend. As the lights from the church blaze out onto the grounds, Brennan begins to sing the opening verse of "Red Roses for Me" to the accompaniment of his melodeon. The final curtain descends.

Red Roses for Me, O'Casey's most autobiographical play, may have been inspired in part by a visit, in 1939, from his old friend and hero James Larkin. The two men had not seen one another for many years. After the first few moments of silence—both too touched by emotion to speak—they spent the rest of the afternoon in excited talk of the past.

The famous 1913 strike of Larkin's Irish Transport and General Workers' Union, of which O'Casey was an enthusiastic member, serves as background to the play. The character Ayamonn reflects many of the experiences, interests, and values of O'Casey himself during this period, when he was deeply under Larkin's influence.

Several other characters in the play also suggest its highly autobiographical nature. Mrs. Breydon has many of the qualities of O'Casey's mother—her humanity, her courage, her love of the musk, fuchsia, and geranium plants that bring a spot of color to the otherwise drab apartment. Roory was based on a tram conductor who first introduced young O'Casey to the ancient nobility of the Gael. The Rector of St. Burnupus is a composite of two rectors from O'Casey's church, St. Barnabas—E.M. Griffin and Harry Fletcher. Both clergymen had been attacked by fundamentalists in the congregation for their liberal views. O'Casey, like Ayamonn, aligned himself with them against the Dowzards and Fosters of the parish.

Sheila is very like a Catholic schoolteacher whom O'Casey met in the St. Lawrence O'Toole club. Her deep antagonism to his left-wing politics, liberal theology, and artistic interests brought about an end to their brief romance.

According to Eileen O'Casey, in her biography *Sean,* Brennan o' the Moore was based on two eccentric personalities who captured O'Casey's imagination. One was an old, Dublin street fiddler O'Casey knew from his childhood. He used to sing hymns about brotherly love, but when children gathered around him, he would lower his voice and order the "little bastards" to get away. O'Casey became acquainted with the other eccentric in Totnes, at the local fair. The man was in a constant panic about the safety of his bank deposits and would badger all listeners for reassurance. O'Casey, who described him as a "wonderful character," used to take notes on his talk.

Characters like Brennan, Roory, and Mullcanny provide a realistic, essentially comic spirit at the beginning of the play. In dialogue characteristically Irish, the belligerent Protestant, the zealous Irish Irelander, and the supercilious atheist keep the battle of the dogmas alive, bickering with the vigor of the streets over issues they really cannot fathom. One of the play's most amusing scenes occurs in the second act when these tough-minded representatives of warring ideologies wrangle fiercely about the theory of evolution as they protect themselves from the mob's stones —by cowering on the floor.

But this realistic, comic atmosphere at the start of the play develops into a poetic, bittersweet vision in which characters and events take on a supernatural dimension. Act III, a visionary fantasy that interrupts the dramatic action of the plot, is responsible in great part for this change of mood by its linking of realistic material with imagery of transformation.

The third act of *Red Roses for Me* reflects that tradition of visionary or prophetic literature that describes the glory of the Lord to which man will be recalled when he attains the state of regeneration. O'Casey's fantasy is particularly reminiscent of Shelley's visionary drama, *Prometheus Unbound*.

Shelley's play describes how the liberation and renewal of mankind is to evolve; its thread of narrative is based on a modified version of the ancient Greek myth of Prometheus. Prometheus gave strength and wisdom to Jupiter in return for a promise that man would remain free. Instead, Jupiter became a despot who imposed every kind of suffering upon his human subjects. In defiance of the despot, Prometheus gave man the gift of fire and the knowledge of art and science that fire makes possible. Retaliating, Jupiter chained Prometheus to the precipice of an icy ravine where a vulture plucked at his heart. Prometheus anathematized his tormentor in one of his moments of agony: "Heap on thy soul, by virtue of this Curse/Ill deeds, then be thou damned. . . ."

Shelley's play opens with Prometheus chained to the precipice, still defying Jupiter after centuries of torture. Panthea and Ione, sisters of Prometheus's wife, Asia, from whom he is separated, try to comfort him. Prometheus has come to pity Jupiter and revokes his curse on the tyrant, saying, "I wish no living thing to suffer."

Mercury and the Furies (described as "thought-executing ministers") come to announce that new tortures are in store for Prometheus if he does not bend to Jupiter. He refuses and is then subjected to terrible scenes of good perverted to evil ends—the mockery of the teachings of Christ, the corrupted fruits of the French Revolution.

At the moment, however, that Prometheus revoked his curse, he set into motion the overthrow of Jupiter and his own liberation. The primal power of the universe, called Demogorgon, drives Jupiter from his throne; and Strength, in the person of Hercules, unbinds Prometheus, who is then reunited with Asia.

There are times when Shelley's writing in *Prometheus Unbound* is somewhat abstract and nebulous, and it is difficult to interpret every sentence on the level of reason. Viewed on a symbolic level, however, Prometheus, the champion of mankind, stands for will, mind, spirit, and imagination; Asia, his wife, for love, beauty, and nature; Panthea, for faith, and Ione, for hope; and the Furies, for the causes of suffering in the world.

Symbolically, Shelley indicated that the mind of man and man himself are enslaved so long as they hate but acquiesce to despots whom they themselves have created or empowered. Man perpetuates evil by his obedience to kings and priests (Jupiter's representatives on earth), who foster convention, fear, hypocrisy, hatred, revenge—and are thereby the chief authors of human misery. Shelley believed that when kings and priests are overthrown by man through a nonviolent act of thought and will, evil must of necessity fall, and man as well as nature will attain a state of regeneration and partake in the glory of the spheres, an existence of intellectual beauty. But man's fate can be created only by man himself.

The fourth and final act of *Prometheus Unbound* is a choral epilogue that might be considered a hymn to deliverance. Despotism is forever at an end. Gentleness, Virtue, Wisdom, and Endurance will keep Evil at bay. Man's victory has been to suffer and forgive, to defy and to love, in Shelley's words:

> To defy Power which seems omnipotent
> To love, and to bear; to hope till Hope creates
> From its own wreck the thing it contemplates;
> Neither to change, nor falter, nor repent; . . .
> This is alone Life, Joy, Empire, and Victory.

These lines of verse might well serve as an epigraph to the third act of *Red Roses for Me*.

In the third act, O'Casey recasts Shelley's dramatic version of the Prometheus myth in terms of Irish history, Celtic myth, and the Christ story. A leader in the strike, Ayamonn is the spiritual heir of James Larkin, whom O'Casey described as "Prometheus Hibernica"

("Irish Prometheus") in his autobiographical *Drums under the Windows*. Ayamonn, a poet as well as a militant, is also identified with Dunn-Bo, a famous hero from Celtic mythology. Ayamonn inspires the slum dwellers to seek liberation and renewal by transcending the environment through spirit and imagination. And he dies for the cause of his fellow workers on the vigil of Easter.

The third act takes place in a dirty street beside the O'Connell Bridge, which arches over the black-looking Liffey River. In the shadows of the decrepit tenements and the brown parapets lounge the slum dwellers, among them Eeada, Dympna, and Finnoola. The women are "dressed so in black that they appear to be enveloped in the blackness of a dark night." All the loungers are exhausted, dispirited, and bitter. They mourn the loss of Ireland's heroic past and find their only recourse in drinking and gambling.

Several characters pass over the bridge. The Inspector and the Rector come on together but hurry away from the sordid scene. The Inspector is disgusted by the shabby people, and the Rector—kindly though he is—senses their hostility toward him and cannot bear "to look twice." They represent state and church, O'Casey's version of Jupiter's representatives on earth.

Half-awake, Dympna, Eeada, and Finnoola begin to reminisce sadly about the past. Finnoola describes her youthful lovers as white-faced and hungry Irish rebels —champions of Ireland—whose shabbiness was threaded from "the garments of Finn MacCool of th' golden hair, Goll MacMorna of th' big blows, Caoilte of th' flyin' feet, an' Oscar of th' invincible spear." (Finn was the central figure of a group of heroic and romantic legends; Goll was a mighty warrior who slew the father of Finn; Caoilte, considered a great poet, once saved Finn by running swiftly throughout Ireland gathering couples of wild beasts and birds; Oscar, the son of Osin and grandson of Finn, was an invincible young warrior, beautiful and gentle.)

Brennan appears on the parapet and begins to sing a gay little love song. During the singing of the last verse, Ayamonn and Roory stroll onstage. The slum dwellers curse the departing Brennan for his frivolity, and they are not responsive to Roory's suggestion that they should have asked for songs about the heroes of old. The 1st, 2nd, and 3rd Men villify Roory as they had Brennan; like the Furies of Shelley, they see only despair, trapped as they are in their moment of misery:

> 1ST MAN (*with a sleepy growl*). Get to hell where gay life has room to move, an' hours to waste, an' white praise is sung to coloured shadows. Time is precious here.
>
> 2ND AND 3RD MEN (*together murmuringly*). Time is precious here.

Hurrying away in disgust, Roory urges Ayamonn to leave these "second-hand ghosts" sprawled on the bridge; but he objects: "Th' leaves an' blossoms have fallen, but th' three [tree] isn't dead."

Ayamonn turns to Eeada, places a comforting hand on her head, and tells her to "think of what we can do to pull down th' banner from dusty bygones, an' fix it up in th' needs an' desires of today." With his plea for her to think, the scene darkens for a few seconds. Ayamonn's head is silhouetted in a streak of sunlight; it looks like "the severed head of Dunn-Bo speaking out of the darkness." (Dunn-Bo, also known as Aengus Og ["the young"] and "Angus of the golden hair," is the Celtic god of youth, love, and beauty as well as song. Although his head was severed in battle, it sang to the Irish warriors as he had promised he would.)

Ayamonn describes what Dublin and its inhabitants could become once again. At first, the dispirited and unbelieving Finnoola tells Ayamonn that even the "Songs of Osheen [Osin] and Sword of Oscar could do nothing to tire this city of its shame." But as Ayamonn continues his description, Finnoola finally "sees" that Dublin—once so drab and miserable—is now "glowin' like a song sung be Osheen himself" and that "the Sword of Light" is shining.

Slowly, the scene brightens, and lovely, vivid colors are heightened by the sun, which now appears in a blue sky. The houses along the river are decked in mauve and burnished bronze. The men previously lounging against them now look like fine, upright, bronze statues, slashed with scarlet; the men near the parapets are similarly transformed, but their clothing is slashed with a vivid green.

Ayamonn points out to the others the changed appearance of the vans and lorries in the Dublin streets visible from the bridge. The city is "in the grip of God!" His poetic, almost rhapsodic, description of the vehicles is similar to passages found in the visionary writings of Ezekiel, Milton, and Shelley—all of them writers in whom O'Casey was deeply versed—when they described the kingdom of heaven.

In Ezekiel the glory of the Lord to which man will be recalled is a gorgeous vision of a spirit that fills a vast "machine" with mysterious wheels. The machine is self-moved because it is pure spirit—a play of magnificent colors in its precious stones and the firmament above it:

> . . . behold one wheel upon the earth by the living creatures. . . . The appearance of the wheels and their work was like unto the colour of a beryl: . . . as it were a wheel in the middle of a wheel . . . And when the living creatures went, the wheels went by them: . . . as the colour of the terrible crystal . . .
>
> Ezekiel 1:15–28

From Ezekiel's vision came Milton's image of the chariot, which is used as a symbol of Christ triumphing spiritually over the rebel angels who have subverted mankind.

. . . forth rush'd with whirl-wind sound
The Chariot of Paternal Deity,
Flashing thick flames, Wheel within Wheel, undrawn,
Itself instinct with Spirit, but convoy'd
By four Cherubic shapes, four Faces each
Had wondrous, as with Stars their bodies all
And Wings were set with Eyes, with Eyes the Wheels
Of Beryl, and careering Fires between;
Over their heads a crystal Firmament . . .

Paradise Lost, Book VI

In Shelley's vision of the future of mankind, the images of wheels and chariots have been transformed into spheres rolling through a firmament instinct with intellectual beauty:

A sphere, which is as many thousand spheres,
Solid as crystal, yet through all its mass
Flow, as through empty space, music and light;
Ten thousand orbs involving and involved,
Purple and azure, white and green and golden,
Sphere within sphere: . . .

Prometheus Unbound, IV, i

And, in O'Casey's vision of what Dublin and its inhabitants could be, we find motor vehicles transformed into images of beauty:

Look! [says Ayamonn] Th' vans an' lorries rattling down th' quays, turned to bronze an' purple by th' sun, look like chariots forging forward to th' battle-front.

The passage finds its analogue in the wheels, chariots, and spheres of visionary writers like Ezekiel, Milton, and Shelley.

Eeada, Dympna, and Finnoola—now comparable to the ideal Panthea, Ione, and Asia—are also transfigured. Eeada and Dympna arise from their groveling postures on the bridge, their faces glowing and dressed in dark-green robes with silvery mantles. Finnoola—or Asia—stands apart from the others. She is dressed in a skirt of a bright green, a white bodice slashed with black, and a flowing silvery scarf.

Ayamonn tells Finnoola that the great dome of the Four Courts, a famous old building in Dublin, looks like "a golden rose in a great bronze bowl"; the Liffey River below it, like "a purple flood, marbled with ripples o' scarlet"; and the sea gulls gliding over the river, like "restless white pearls astir on a royal breast." He says that the city is "in the grip of God." Its transformation began with Ayamonn's telling Eeada to "think of what we can do," or as Shelley said, "to hope till Hope creates/ From its own wreck the thing it contemplates."

All join in singing a militant workers' song. Ayamonn and Finnoola begin to dance. She is in a golden pool of light; he in a violet colored shadow. Now and again, they change their movements so that she is in the shadow and he in the light. The radiance of O'Casey's dance scene suggests Shelley's "Light of Life" and the Chorus of Spirits in *Prometheus Unbound*, where love is identified with dazzling light and the harmony of dance. Everyone joins in singing a song of admiration for Ireland, for joy, and for the imagination.

As the marching feet of soldiers sent to prevent the strike are heard offstage, the scene darkens. Ayamonn says that he must leave to join his comrades for the sake of a future generation as glorious as those of the

past. The act ends as it began, with a gray sky, decrepit houses, and the black river; but, as we have
already seen in the last act, the slum dwellers no
longer have their look of stony, frozen resignation and
despair: they have joined the strikers. Like Prometheus, a champion of mankind, Ayamonn has inspired
the slum dwellers to see a shilling in the shape of a
new world.

O'Casey's view about the way to resist the forces of
evil was very different from that of Shelley. Ayamonn's
active leadership in the union strike indicates the po-
larity between O'Casey's dialectics of struggle and
Shelley's nonviolent radicalism. Prometheus remains
separated from Asia until capable of renouncing his
curse; Ayamonn is separated from Finnoola to join his
comrades in resisting the oppressor. Where Shelley
emphasized the psychological transcending of "the
painted veil of life," O'Casey emphasized the social
transforming of life into "the way where the redder
roses grow."

Ayamonn fights against the corruption of individual
integrity that results in a philosophy like Sheila's of
each man for himself. He fights, and dies, for the
rights of the individual within the group. The association of Ayamonn with Prometheus, Dunn-Bo, and the
martyred Christ give to the character an epic, noble,
and religious stature that transcends the immediate
background of the 1913 strike.

O'Casey developed the "Red Roses" of the title in
various ways. It figures first as a Lancastrian emblem
during the scene when Ayamonn and his mother are
reciting lines from Shakespeare's play. The image re-
curs in Ayamonn's song of love. It becomes all the
creative activities that uplift man when Ayamonn tells
Sheila that he will tread where the "redder roses" grow
even if there are thorns. At the end of the play, when
Sheila places the crimson roses on the breast of the

corpse, they symbolize the higher qualities of the human spirit—courage, loyalty, integrity—embodied in the young martyr. The red roses come to symbolize the very blood of human kinship that transcends all else. By comparison, the refurbished statue of the Virgin Mary—also a symbol of human potential—is too limited in scope to help her "poor children," the slum dwellers who venerate her; the Virgin can show them only "a cheerier way to die."

On 15 March 1943, *Red Roses for Me* was produced at Dublin's Olympia Theatre, the first O'Casey premiere in his native country in seventeen years. Its success was only moderate. Apparently the production staff had a difficult time handling the third-act fantasy in a way that would integrate it with the rest of the play. Many critics deplored O'Casey's continued experimentation in dramatic fantasy when they felt his real gift lay in realism.

In March 1946 Bronson Albery produced the play at the Embassy Theatre in London. It was directed by Ria Mooney, formerly a member of the Abbey Theatre repertory company, who had come over from Dublin with several members of the original cast. Despite the difficulties in staging the third act, James Redfern (an important critic from the *Spectator*) considered the production "one of the most attractive plays to be seen in London at the present moment." Several London critics commented on the outstanding performances of Eddie Bryne as Brennan o' the Moore and Maureen Pryor as Sheila Moornen. O'Casey, who had not seen one of his plays in production for several years, was persuaded by his wife to attend the performance. He was delighted by Bryne's characterization of Brennan.

In the 1955–56 season, Gordon W. Pollock produced the play in New York at the Booth Theater: it was directed by John O'Shaughnessy and choreographed by Anna Sokolow. (The last O'Casey play seen on Broadway had been *Within the Gates* in 1934.) Several critics noted the outstanding performances of E. G. Marshall as Brennan o' the Moore, Kevin McCarthy as Ayamonn, and Eileen Crowe (of the Abbey Theatre) as Mrs. Breydon.

Harold Clurman of *The Nation*, who had given the play a very favorable review, expressed the hope that it might be performed in an Off-Broadway theater, away from the competitive market, which requires spectacular hits for adequate financing. He felt that "there is a significant audience" for the play in New York.

Clurman's wish came true six years later: in 1961, *Red Roses for Me* was produced at the Greenwich Mews Theater in Greenwich Village. Almost all reviewers singled out Martyn Green, the English actor, for his excellent performance of Brennan o' the Moore.

Since 1961, there has been no noteworthy performance of *Red Roses for Me*, either in this country or abroad. This is indeed a shame, for the poetry and fantasy in the play absolutely require stage presentation.

Cock-a-doodle Dandy

Cock-a-doodle Dandy was produced in 1949 by an amateur group in England. The main plot is about the repressive forces that attempt to control the lives of the young people in an Irish village; a subplot concerns a threatened strike by peat-bog workers and a second subplot, the unsuccessful attempt of a dying girl to achieve a miraculous cure at Lourdes in France.

The three scenes of the play take place in a garden in front of Michael Marthraun's house, in the village Nyadanave—morning, noon, and dusk of the same day. Although no time for the dramatic action is fixed, O'Casey probably meant it to be the late 1940s, when the play was written. According to the stage directions for Scene I, the garden is rough and uncared for. Surrounding the garden is a stone wall, three or four feet high, with a wooden gate. To the left, a little way from the gate, stand a clump of sunflowers with petals "like rays from an angry sun."

The house, the front of which is visible to the left of the sunflowers, is painted black. The porch is supported by twisted, wooden pillars that look like snakes and are connected with latticework shaped like noughts and crosses. Porch, pillars, and latticework are painted white, which dazzles in contrast to the black house. The framework of the window above the porch is slightly crooked, and the sashwork holding the glass is twisted into irregular lines; sashwork and frame are brilliant red.

Some distance from the porch is an urn, which holds a "stand-offish, cynical looking evergreen." Near the garden wall, the Irish Tricolour flutters from a flag-pole.

The day is a brilliant one. The grass has turned to a deep yellow hue from the sun. In the distance, beyond the wall, a bog of rich purple color, daubed here and there with black patches, can be seen. The sky above is a silvery gray. In the distance, an accordion can be heard playing a dance tune.

A few minutes after the curtain rises, a huge rooster comes dancing in around the house, circles the urn, and disappears around the house as the music stops. The Cock is of a deep black plumage, yellow feet and ankles, bright-green wings, and a stiff cloak falling like a tail behind him. A big crimson crest flowers over his face and crimson flaps hang from his jaws; his face has the look of "a cynical jester."

Michael Marthraun, a farmer who is now the owner of a lucrative peat-producing bog, comes onstage with Sailor Mahan, the owner of a fleet of trucks that carries the peat from bog to town. Michael, who is over sixty, is clean-shaven, lean, and grim-looking; Mahan, about fifty, has a short, pointed beard, a ruddy, rather good-looking face, and a serene countenance.

Michael tells Mahan that the house is full of evil whispers, which began when his daughter, Loreleen, from a first marriage, returned to the village after having lived in London. According to Michael, whenever she walks by the holy objects in the house, a wind blows the pictures out of their frames and turns their faces to the wall; and, once, the statue of St. Patrick tried to hit her with his crosier and fell flat on its face when it missed.

Mahan registers some disbelief, but Michael goes on to say that his second wife, Lorna, is also involved in the disorder of the house—he once saw gay-colored horns branching from her head. Michael resents his wife's love of frivolities such as gay dress and dancing, but Mahan retorts that he should never have married so much younger a woman who was pressured into the match by her father, the priest, and Michael himself. Michael's rationale is that he gave Lorna's poverty-stricken father fifty pounds so that her younger sister Julia, who is dying, can make the trip to the shrine Lourdes for a miraculous cure. All that he ever got in return, says Michael, was a worthless bog. Mahan points out that since peat came into its own as a fuel, the bog has become very valuable and Michael, now a rich man and the "fair-haired boy of the clergy," has been made a councillor and a justice of the peace.

The two begin to argue about which of them will pay the additional shilling in wages the peat-bog workers are demanding. Loreleen, Michael's daughter, appears in the doorway just as the crow of the Cock is heard in the distance. A very attractive, intelligent-looking young girl, Loreleen is dressed in a dark-green dress with dark-red flashes on the bodice and side of the skirt. Her hat, of a brighter green than the dress, has on it a scarlet ornament, suggestive of a cock's crimson crest.

The two men continue their haggling about the shilling much to Loreleen's amused contempt. She starts to walk out of the gate. The First Rough Fellow, hurrying through from the pathway, pushes her aside until, noticing how pretty she is, he says with excitement: "It isn't here you should be, lost among th' rough stones, th' twisty grass, an' th' moody misery o' th' brown bog. . . ." And he tells her to wait for him until he finishes talking to the two men. Close on his heels follows the Second Rough Fellow, who is also smitten by Loreleen and says: "Arra, what winsome wind blew such a flower into this dhread, dhried-up desert?" And he asks her to wait for him. But, Loreleen, saying she is not for them, goes out of the gate and down the path.

The two Rough Fellows are peasants who work Michael's bog. They have come to warn him and Mahan that if one or the other does not give the men the additional shilling, there will be a strike. The Second Rough Fellow asks Michael how he expects the men to live on their meager paychecks. Michael's answer is that they must look to the *Rerum Novarum* (a papal document that enjoins obedience on the part of workers toward employers).

The Rough Fellows hurry out to catch up with Loreleen but suddenly stop and stare ahead of them in fear. They report that a cloud is closing in on her, lightning is whirling around her head, her whole figure is rippling, and she has taken on the look of "a fancy-bred fowl." Frightened by the sight, the Rough Fellows swear to heed the warning of the local priest about the evil powers inherent in womankind, and they hurry off in the opposite direction.

Michael believes that Loreleen's reported transformation proves her an evil spirit, but Mahan dismisses the Rough Fellows as drunk. Michael tells a local tale about another evil woman, the Widow Malone, who could turn herself into a hare and was found bleeding to death after her leg had been snapped off by a pursuing dog. The men return to their argument about the shilling, until a frustrated Mahan accuses Michael of being ready enough to waste good money on an expensive top hat so that he can greet the President of Ireland, who plans to visit the village.

Shanaar walks into the garden. A very old man with

a wrinkled face and a long, rather dirty white beard, he is dressed in shabby peasant garb. Shanaar corroborates Michael's belief in evil spirits that can manifest themselves in the most seemingly innocent things —a bee, a bird, a beautiful woman—but that can be recognized because they have "no behinds."

To prove that birds can be evil incarnate, Shanaar tells of a cuckoo that tempted a holy brother into a glade where he saw a naked woman bathing. She persuaded him (in return for her favors) to steal money from a rich man whom he subsequently killed; he was caught and sentenced to hang. On the scaffold, while the poor brother sobbed, the spectators could hear the mocking laughter of a girl and the calling of a cuckoo. Just as Shanaar is finishing his story, the sobbing of a man, the laughing of a girl, and the calling of a cuckoo can be heard. Mahan and Michael sit up stiffly in their chairs, but Shanaar tells them to pretend not to hear.

He tells another local tale of an evil bird, a corncrake that tempted a young lad to steal. The lad ended up in the reformatory, his mother died of a broken heart, and his father took to drink. During his recital, the call of a corncrake is heard. Even a hen can be an evil spirit, says Shanaar, but it can be overcome: "The one thing to do, if youse have the knowledge, is to parley with th' hen in a Latin dissertation. If among th' fowl there's an illusion of a hen from Gehenna, it won't endure th' Latin."

Suddenly a commotion is heard from the house: a loud cackling mixed with the crow of a cock, the breaking of china, and the cries of frightened women. Marion, a maid in the Marthraun household, comes rushing out on the porch, terrified. About twenty and very attractive, she wears a maid's uniform; but around her head, instead of the typical maid's cap, she wears a scarf-bandeau ornamented with silver stripes, joined in the center above her forehead with an enameled stone, each stripe extending along the bandeau as far as either ear.

Marion tells the men that some kind of bird is clawing the holy pictures and pecking at Michael's top hat. Michael orders her to get Father Domineer to help. As she runs out of the gate, she bumps into the Messenger, who is coming in; he is a handsome young man named Robin Adair. He wears a silver-gray coat and trousers, a green beret and green sandals; on the right side of the coat is a flash of a pair of scarlet wings. The Messenger and Marion are lovers. She explains to him that the house has been invaded by some kind of bird, which is destroying everything. After handing a telegram to Michael, who puts it into his pocket without looking at its contents, the Messenger goes into the house to investigate the trouble.

The head of the Cock, thrust through the window, lets out a violent crow. Michael and Mahan, in the garden, fall flat as if in a dead faint. From under cover of the garden wall, Shanaar intones fervently: "*Oh, rowelum randee, horrida aidus, sed spero spiro specialli spam. . . . Oh, dana eirebus, heniba et galli scatterum in multus parvum avic asthorum!*" The Cock's head disappears, a louder commotion is heard and then all is silent. The Messenger comes out, calmly leading the Cock by a green ribbon tied to a silver staff.

The Messenger tells the frightened men there is no reason to fear the Cock. Michael's pretty wife, Lorna, leans through the house window. She is very anxious at the moment. The Messenger explains to her that the women frightened the Cock with their cries: ". . . if only you'd given him your lily-white hand, he'd have led you through a wistful an' wondherful dance." Pacified, Marion now pets the bird. The Messenger tells it,

"Go on, comrade, lift up th' head an' clap th' wings, black cock, an' crow!" The Cock crows lustily, and the Messenger leads it out of the garden.

Marion mocks the frightened men and enters the house. Shanaar warns Michael to beware of women like Marion, barking cats, meowing dogs, and "the scourge of materialism" in the country, completing his tirade with "th' coruscatin' conduct in th' dance-halls [which] is completin' th' ruin." After the old man leaves with Michael's blessing, Mahan curses him as a danger to the community.

The nervous Michael orders Marion to bring out a bottle of whiskey. The men are very taken by her pert ways. While she is in the house, Mahan says he would be willing to welcome Marion even if he saw her with Shanaar's vision of "horns growin' out of her head!" And Michael agrees. When Marion returns with the bottle, she finds the two men looking straight in front of them with silly grins on their faces. The ornament Marion wears around her head has separated into two parts, each of which branches over her head, forming two horns that seem to sprout from her forehead. She offers to let the men kiss her, but when they lean toward her in great excitement, they notice the horns and flip back on their seats, terrified at the sight. At Lorna's call, Marion returns to the house, puzzled at their strange behavior.

Julia, Lorna's younger sister, is borne on a stretcher along the path by the two Rough Fellows. Her face is like a sad, yellowish mask, pierced by wide eyes surrounded by dark circles. She is followed by her father, who looks straight ahead in a passive and stony stare. Lorna and Marion, who have come out of the house, run over to wish Julia well on her journey to Lourdes.

The parish priest, Father Domineer, hurries into the garden. A tall, rather heavily built man, he tries "to smile now, but crack his mouth as he will, the tight, surly lines of his face refuse to furnish one. . . . his hard head is covered with a soft . . . black hat." Father Domineer promises that Julia will come back miraculously cured, and the procession leaves. The scene ends with the sound of a crowd singing a hymn to the Queen of Heaven.

The staging of Scene II is the same as for Scene I, but the sun "isn't quite so bright and determined" as before. In the distance, the music of the same hymn can be heard. After a few minutes Lorna and Marion come onstage and enter the house. They are followed by Michael and Mahan, who now begin to argue about whether or not heaven listens to the prayers of unimportant people like the villagers. Michael is convinced that heaven does, not so Mahan.

The Messenger comes into the garden and ventures his opinion that the clergy most honors the man who gives the largest contribution. Furiously Michael retorts: "With that kinda talk, we won't be able soon to sit steady on our chairs"; and the chair on which he is sitting collapses. When Mahan adds that "the way things are goin' we won't be able much longer to sit serene on our chairs," his chair also collapses.

Marion comes out of the house and, noticing the broken chairs, scolds Michael for taking them when he knew they were unsteady and meant only for decoration. When the Messenger embraces her, Michael reminds him that he has already spent time in jail for public kissing. Notwithstanding the implied threat, the Messenger kisses Marion. Then he asks if anyone has seen the Cock, which has disappeared. In the distance a loud, exultant crow is heard, and the Messenger goes off toward the sound as Marion enters the house with the broken chairs.

The crowing has terrified Michael and Mahan, who decide to have a drink to steady their nerves. As he grasps the bottle, Michael repeats that there are "sinisther enchantments" all around them. He tilts the bottle over, but nothing spills out. When Mahan tries, the bottle turns a glowing red color. Michael believes the bottle has been bewitched and cautions Mahan that virtuous men must think about only four things: ". . . hell, heaven, death, an' th' judgement."

As they argue about how to rid themselves of the now demonized bottle, a Porter appears on the path, carrying a parcel wrapped in brown paper. It contains the new top hat ordered by Michael after the Cock destroyed his old one. But, according to the Porter, the Civic Guards, who were shooting at the Cock, hit the top hat by mistake. He places it on the garden wall. A shot rings out and the hat is knocked from the wall to the road.

The Sergeant of the Civic Guards runs along the path, asking excitedly if anyone has seen the Cock, which he shot at three times. On the third shot, he reports, everything went dark, then came a blinding flash of red lightning, and seconds after "there was the demonised Cock changin' himself into a silken glossified tall-hat [top hat]." The listeners move quickly away from the top hat, which still lies on the road.

When the Sergeant raises his gun to his shoulder to demonstrate how he aimed at the Cock, there are a few moments of darkness, then a flash of lightning; the hat disappears, and the Cock, crowing lustily, stands in its place. When the regular light returns, both the Cock and top hat are gone. Michael tells Mahan that maybe now he will believe the words of Shanaar about the evil spirits in the land. The Sergeant blames the women, who must be prevented in the future from gallivanting after the men and forced to stay in the house where they belong. Michael adds that there must also be an end to minds that babble about books. When the Sergeant tries to get a drink from the bottle, he discovers it is red-hot.

A Bellman appears, shouting that everyone must get inside because the Cock is coming in the shape of a woman. Michael orders everyone to sit on the ground instead and pretend indifference to the Cock, should it appear. He encourages a shaky but compliant Mahan to sing an old sailors' chantey. Loreleen comes into the garden, a golden light following her, and asks what is wrong with everyone. Lorna and Marion come out of the house, dressed in costume for a dance to be held that evening.

Lorna gets into a heated argument with Michael about the top hat, which she insists is not in the house but has disappeared. Mahan prevents him from striking her. Marion comes out of the house with the top hat in her hands, much to Michael's utter amazement. Lorna gets the "demonized" bottle of whiskey so that she can have a drink and (with no difficulty) pours some into a glass. She drinks happily to "Th' Cock-a-doodle Dandy" and persuades the others to join her.

The Messenger appears and begins to play his accordion. A change in mood comes over the group. Mahan and Michael, each of whom now offers to pay the additional shilling to the workers, are serene and happy. The women invite the men to dance with them. As they begin to dance with one another, the ornaments on the heads of Marion and Lorna change into graceful, curving horns, and the cocklike crest on Loreleen's hat rises higher.

As they are dancing in high spirits, Father Domineer rushes into the garden; a long peal of loud thunder, followed by a lusty crow, is heard. Father Domineer demands that the dancers stop their wickedness immediately and ask his pardon. All are contrite except Loreleen. Father Domineer has come to order Mahan to fire one of his workers, who is living "in sin" with a woman. Mahan refuses because the man is one of his best drivers. The worker of whom they speak comes

into the garden to tell Mahan that the bog workers
have gone on strike and there is no peat to load into
the trucks. (The telegram delivered to Michael—
which he never read—was their last warning.) Father
Domineer tells the worker he must leave the woman
immediately. When he refuses, he hits him violently
on the side of the head. The scene ends with Mahan's
solemn announcement that the worker has been killed
by the blow.

The third and last scene takes place in the garden,
early in the evening. The big sunflowers have turned
into "a solemn black" and the house looks more sinister
than ever. In the distance, the sound of a drumming,
occasionally pierced by the shrill notes of a fife, can be
heard. Mahan is sitting at the table, busily working at
his calculations. Lorna and Marion are leaning against
the wall near the gate.

All of the villagers, led by Father Domineer, are out
in pursuit of the Cock. Marion says, "Th' place'll lose
its brightness if th' Cock's killed." And Lorna wonders:
"How can they desthroy a thing they say themselves is
not of this world?" The Cock glides into the garden,
weaving his way between Mahan and Lorna; he circles the garden and disappears around the end of the
house.

Father Domineer, accompanied by Michael and
One-eyed Larry, a peasant lad and potential sacristan,
comes into the garden to purge the house of its evil
influences. One-eyed Larry carries bell, book, and
candle. They enter the house.

Marion notices a girl running toward them. It is
Loreleen, pursued by a hostile mob, which has taken
exception to her gay appearance and open manner.
After Loreleen has found safety in the garden, Marion
and Lorna run down the road to upbraid the mob.
While they are gone, Mahan warns Loreleen that she
must leave the village for her safety. Since Michael has

confiscated her savings and will not return them, Mahan offers her money to go away if she will meet him that evening in some private place.

As they are speaking, the house shakes, a sound of objects moving and crockery breaking comes from it, several flashes of lightning appear and the flagpole wags drunkenly back and forth. One-eyed Larry comes rushing out, just in time to see Mahan attempting to embrace a reluctant Loreleen.

The house shakes worse than before and seems to lurch over to one side, the flagpole continues to wag furiously, and blue lightning flashes from the windows. Larry says that they are successfully exorcizing evil spirits like Kissalass, Velvet-thighs, Reedabuck, Dancesolong, and Sameagain. The house gives another ominous lurch, the flagpole falls flat, blue and red lightning flash from the window, a peal of thunder sounds, and then deathly silence.

Both limping, Father Domineer and Michael come through the now-lurching porch, both with blackened faces and tattered clothing. Father Domineer announces that the house is exorcised of all evil spirits— including "Anticlericus," "Secularius," and "Odeonius" (hedonism). He orders the women into the house— their proper place—to clean up the wreckage, but Loreleen refuses to join them. When Father Domineer is apprised by Michael of his daughter's many evil thoughts that come from her books, he sends Larry to get the books—as it turns out a life of Voltaire and *Ulysses* by Joyce. But Loreleen grabs the books from One-eyed Larry and runs out of the garden with them.

As Loreleen disappears from sight, the Cock suddenly springs over the wall. The Sergeant appears, in hot pursuit. The Cock pirouettes around for some moments, then the scene darkens, two shots are heard, there is a clash of thunder, and the garden is light again. Both Father Domineer and the Cock are gone.

Michael and Mahan, complaining that they have been mortally wounded by the gunshot, are lying on the ground. One-eyed Larry says that Father Domineer has been carried off by the Cock. Mahan pulls a bullet as big "as a cigar" out of his pocket—presumably it has gone through him and Michael with no effect whatsoever.

After another futile discussion about which of them will pay the extra shilling—each denies having ever made the offer—Mahan leaves in anger. When Lorna tells Michael he could well afford the extra amount, he shakes her for daring to mention his private accounts. The sound of a high wind is heard; it causes Michael to rush back and forth toward the gate as he fights its propulsion.

Hanging on to his trousers, which are being blown about, One-eyed Larry rushes into the garden to announce that Father Domineer was carried home safely by some bird but no one can agree what kind. Also propelled by the wind, the Bellman comes on stage—only the collar and one sleeve left on his coat. He warns that the Cock is on its way. Cap and trousers gone, the Sergeant is pushed by the wind into the garden. He explains that they were ripped off by a blast of wind, and he enters the house to borrow clothing from Michael.

The sound of the wind rises even higher, carrying in it an occasional moan. The Messenger walks in and sits down on the wall. Michael, the Bellman, and One-eyed Larry grip the waistbands of their trousers and begin to make sudden jerky movements as if dragged back and forth by an invisible force. The Messenger begins to play his accordion in mocking accompaniment.

Suddenly Father Domineer appears, accompanied by the sound of a gust of wind, fierce and shrill, which declines into a sad wail and then ceases altogether. He calls on the men to fight the Cock. In the distance, the sound of fifing and drumming along with booing is heard.

Shanaar appears on the pathway, followed by the two Rough Fellows, who drag Loreleen between them; her clothes are awry and blood is on her face. They tell Father Domineer they roughed up her and Mahan because they caught them together, and he "a married man . . . thrying to put an arm around her." Assured that Mahan—a good knight of "St. Columbanus"—has not been hurt but is safe, sound, and in bed with his wife, Father Domineer berates Loreleen for having tried to seduce the man. When she explains that he gave her money so that she could leave the village, Father Domineer asks for it. The Rough Fellows say they ripped up the tainted bills, and they twist Loreleen's arms when she insists that they pocketed it instead. The Messenger threatens to twist their necks if they do not loosen Loreleen from their grasp.

After castigating the Messenger for his interference, Father Domineer banishes Loreleen from the village. As she starts slowly down the road—with neither shoes nor money to help her on her way—Lorna comes out of the house and joins her. "Lift up your head, lass," she says, "we go not towards an evil, but leave an evil behind us." They walk out together. All the others exit except Michael, the Messenger, and Shanaar.

Marion comes out of the house, prepared to follow the other women, and invites the willing Messenger to join them in exile. Julia comes in on her stretcher, as sick as when she left for Lourdes. The Messenger tells her that Lorna has gone "to a place where life resembles life more than it does here." When she asks his blessing, he tells her to be brave. As the Messenger leaves, Michael asks him what he should do now that he is alone. The answer is "Die." Singing a song, the Messenger walks offstage as Michael leans forward on the table and buries his head in his hands.

In her biography *Sean*, Eileen O'Casey wrote that her husband was always excited about writing a new play and would often sing a good deal—"as if the rhythm, mostly of Irish folk-songs, helped his thought." He was particularly excited when he was writing *Cock-a-doodle Dandy* because he had resolved to employ fantastic elements throughout an entire play.

In a 1958 article intended to introduce the first American production of *Cock-a-doodle Dandy*, O'Casey discussed his new dramatic approach as well as the themes of the play (*see* "Cock-a-doodle Doo," in *Blasts and Benedictions*). He said that for him realism was not enough, and he had tried to incorporate in the play the comic, the serious, and the poetic imagination. The play is symbolical; although the action manifests itself in Ireland, the spirit it describes is to be found anywhere in the world: ". . . the fight made by the many to drive the joy of life from the hearts of men; the fight against this fight to vindicate the right of the joy of life to live courageously in the hearts of men."

O'Casey accused many different groups of trying to frustrate this joy of life and to shout down any new artistic effort—in the U.S.A., in the U.S.S.R, in England, and especially in Ireland. They should be violently fought whether the groups are poets, playwrights, priests, peasants, prime ministers, or proletarians.

He went on to explain that the Cock in the play symbolizes the "joyful, active spirit of life" as it weaves a way through the Irish scene—for it was through an Irish scene that his imagination could best weave its way. The Cock dances and crows among the young and the souls zealous for life, and it brings consternation and hatred to those who want to deny life and keep the mind in the dark.

O'Casey said further that in spite of the fanciful nature of the play and Irish critics notwithstanding, many of the incidents are factual: the priest's blow that killed the worker; the mauling of the gay young girl by the rough fellows; the illegality of any public display of affection; the feeding on popular superstition by the old, menacing fool; and the never-ending quest for money to the detriment of all other human values.

Despite the fear in the play, O'Casey felt that there was also courage, reason, and laughter. And he ended his article with a quote from Yeats's poem "Why should the heart take fright?"

> Lift up the head
> And clap the wings,
> Red Cock, and crow!

These words, which obviously inspired O'Casey in his conception of the play, are paraphrased by the Messenger in the first scene, when he introduces the harmless Cock to the women.

In form, *Cock-a-doodle Dandy* is a comic fantasy with overtones of farce and, at the same time, a savage satire. The fantastic figure of the Cock is responsible for the supernatural stage business in the play: spells are cast on holy objects, chairs, flagpoles, and houses collapse; a whiskey bottle goes dry and glows red hot; sounds of the cuckoo and the corncrake are heard; cigar-shaped bullets course through human bodies without leaving a trace; and a powerful wind blows off clothing—selectively. The Cock itself can take the shape of a top hat or a beautiful woman.

The Cock—with his look of a "cynical jester"—is also a symbol of the sexual instinct, which has been thwarted by the puritanism of priest and politician. The symbolic headgear of Loreleen, Lorna, and Marion associates them with the life force of the Cock. The Messenger, Robin Adair (a figure from popular ballad associated with Maid Marion) is also a votary of the bird.

During the second scene, the women lure Michael and Mahan away from their bickering about profits and persuade them to join in a dance, symbolically a dance of life. (The headgear the women wear rises during the sequence.) But Father Domineer, the symbol of life denial, rushes onstage to the accompaniment of thunder and, in his usual domineering manner, shames everyone except Loreleen into asking his pardon for that "devil's dance."

The ferocious puritanism of Father Domineer has not so much killed the sexual instinct in the villagers as frustrated and misdirected it. His parishoners can never react naturally and joyously to sex. The Rough Fellows lust after Loreleen and see her as transformed into the Cock, for them the embodiment of the devil. Shanaar also has sex on the brain in an evil and stupid way with his tales of nude women seducing holy brothers who end up on the gibbet. Even Mahan, the most sympathetic of the older men, tries to use money badly needed by Loreleen to coerce her into intimacy. The consequence of Father Domineer's attitude is that he, albeit unintentionally, kills a worker who refuses to give up a woman with whom he is living "in sin."

The death-blow changes the mood from comic fantasy to bitter satire and foreshadows the end of the play. Loreleen will be beaten by the mob and banished from the village; the other young people will follow her into exile; and the Cock will be defeated by the spirit of Father Domineer.

In the figure of Michael and his celebrated top hat, to be worn for the visit of the country's President,

O'Casey was satirizing the Catholic-bourgeois-capital-ist who, allied with the clergy, has become the greatest power in theocratic Ireland. The Michaels and the Father Domineers are responsible for what O'Casey considered the spiritual ills of the island: prejudice, ignorance, superstition, hatred, fear, and cruelty. After the young people go into exile seeking freedom, Mi-chael is left with his appetite for money, his sense of sexual sin, and his loneliness.

Ultimately, the Cock symbolizes a state of mind. The gay cockerel can scourge the fools of the village as an avenging jester (O'Casey himself?), but he cannot defeat the unholy alliance of biretta and top hat when its power is sanctioned by the stupidity of the mob.

Cock-a-doodle Dandy always remained O'Casey's favorite play; at this writing, it has never been pro-duced in Ireland. It has usually been considered one of his most difficult plays to stage because of the fantastic incidents.

First produced in Newcastle-upon-Tyne at the Peo-ples Theatre in December 1949, *Cock-a-doodle Dandy* opened to American audiences in February 1950, in Dallas, Texas, at the Arena Stage in a production by Margo Jones.

In a *New York Times* article (11 January 1953), Brooks Atkinson excoriated the theater industry for spending thousands of dollars for rubbish but nothing for O'Casey. He pointed out that *Cock-a-doodle Dandy* had been available for production for four years, and he described the play as O'Casey's finest achievement since he abandoned the realistic form.

In November 1958, *Cock-a-doodle Dandy* finally opened to New Yorkers at the Off-Broadway Carnegie Hall Playhouse. While Atkinson (*New York Times*, 23 December 1958) was pleased with Carlo Mazzone's performance as the Cock, he was very critical of the

leading actors Will Geer and Ian Martin, whose performances of Michael and Mahan were flawed in
characterization. Atkinson ended by saying that although the performance was imperfect, it accom-
plished one excellent thing: it got the play on the
stage. Eileen O'Casey, who had come over from Torquay, England, for the opening, did not think herself
that it was a good production for what is admittedly a
demanding play.

On 7 September 1959, *Cock-a-doodle Dandy* was
performed at the Edinburgh Festival in Scotland. As
described by London correspondent W. A. Darlington,
in a special to the *New York Times* (8 September
1959), a moving and imaginative production of the
play saved the theater division of the festival, which
had been sagging badly. The triumphant performance
was given by the English Stage Company, of the
Royal Court Theatre in London, headed by George
Devine. Darlington felt that the play had been un-
deservedly neglected. He wrote that O'Casey is everywhere acclaimed a genius but his freedom of expression has made him an anathema in Ireland, and his
subject matter does not interest English managers. He
ended the article with the hope that, at seventy-nine,
O'Casey could have another taste of the success that
was his with the earliest plays.

The Edinburgh production then went on to London,
where it had a successful run of several weeks.
O'Casey, who had not been in a London theater for
years, accepted an invitation to see his favorite work in
its first major production, so many years after it had
been published (1949). He was very pleased by the
performance, one of the last he ever attended.

In January 1969, *Cock-a-doodle Dandy* was staged
at the Lyceum Theater in New York. Clive Barnes, in
a review for the *New York Times* (21 January 1969),
took exception to what he considered O'Casey's obses-

sive anticlericalism and to his "stage-Irish," which he believed becomes a caricature of itself. He did admit, however, that the actors might be in part to blame. He concluded by saying that *Cock-a-doodle Dandy* is far from a perfect play, and far from perfectly done in this production, but that it remained one of the more stimulating evenings on Broadway.

In March of 1976, *Cock-a-doodle Dandy* was produced at the WPA Theatre Off-Broadway in New York City. The production was one of the best ever seen in this country since the play was first done in 1958 in a basement theater in Carnegie Hall. The cast was generally good, but special honors go to S. G. Benzali and Terence M. Sullivan, who played, respectively, the demanding roles of Sailor Mahan and Michael Marthraun. The director emphasized O'Casey's sympathetic attitude toward women in a way which had not been previously done. Eileen O'Casey, the playwright's widow, was also present.

Sean O'Casey
EDIZIONI PAOLINE, ROME

The Shadow of a Gunman, the first O'Casey play to be accepted by the prestigious Abbey Theatre, helped to save that company from imminent bankruptcy. Lady Gregory wrote of the premiere performance of the play, which is set in the time of the Anglo-Irish War, that "all the political points [were] taken up with delight by a big audience." In this scene from the 1971 Abbey production of *The Shadow of a Gunman*, Seumas Shields (Philip O'Flynn) and Donal Davoren (Bob Carlile) look apprehensively toward the back alley, where a volley of shots has just been fired.
IRISH TOURIST BOARD

Barry Fitzgerald appeared in the role of Captain Boyle, the wastrel "paycock," in various Abbey Theatre productions of *Juno and the Paycock*. His interpretation of the part was fantastically comic. "Even his face, alternately querulous and alarmed, was an essential part of . . . Fitzgerald's portrayal [which] made of Boyle one of the theater's masterpieces" (Brooks Atkinson).
CULVER PICTURES, INC.

The Plough and the Stars, probably O'Casey's most controversial play among Irish theatergoers, depicts the heroes of Ireland's bloody Easter Rebellion in an antiheroic light. O'Casey was bitterly criticized by critics and public alike for his "betrayal" of the "good Irish people." Pictured in this scene from John Ford's 1936 film version of *The Plough and the Stars* are Mrs. Gogan (Una O'Connor; seated), Uncle Peter (J. M. Kerrigan), Jack Clitheroe (Preston Foster), Nora (Barbara Stanwyck), and Fluther Good (Barry Fitzgerald).
CULVER PICTURES, INC.

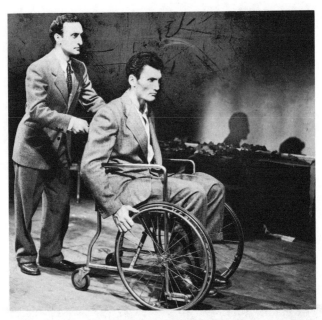

The blind Teddy Foran (Fred Porcelli) wheels the para-
lyzed war veteran Harry Heegan (Jack Palance) around
the dance hall in this scene from the Interplayers' 1949 New
York production of *The Silver Tassie*. A play about "the
aftermath of adventure and the ease with which the healthy
reject the maimed, and edit them into oblivion for their
own peace of mind" (Irving Wardle), *The Silver Tassie*
was a milestone in O'Casey's career in both its subject matter and its expressionistic technique.
CULVER PICTURES, INC.

Lillian Gish as Jannice, a young prostitute, and Bramwell
Fletcher as The Dreamer, a poet of humanistic vision, in
the 1934 New York premiere of *Within the Gates* at the
National Theatre. A play that presents church and state as
forces that repress rather than celebrate life, *Within the
Gates* was to tour the United States and Canada but was
banned by the first city of the tour, Boston, in response to
pressure from various religious groups.
CULVER PICTURES, INC.

In 1966 the Berliner Ensemble produced *Purple Dust*, in German, under the direction of Hans Georg Simmgen. Pictured here are Gisela May as Souhaun and Hermann Hiesgen as Poges. Comic and rhapsodic in style, universal in theme, *Purple Dust* illustrates O'Casey's basic convictions "that life should be lived joyously by everyone; that freedom includes . . . freedom from stuffy conventions, freedom from social humbug of all kinds" (Brooks Atkinson).
SAEGER

James-Ivers O'Connor as the Cock and Bonnie Brewster as Loreleen, in the WPA Theater production of *Cock-a-doodle Dandy*, offered in New York City in 1976. A blend of comic fantasy and realism, *Cock-a-doodle Dandy* was O'Casey's favorite play. An enchanted cock, symbol of the life force, tries to fight the bigotry, superstition, and puritanism of a little town in Ireland. As O'Casey pointed out, the tyranny and hate that infect this "nest of knaves" can be found in many places around the globe.

ROGER GREENAWALT, NEW YORK

OTHER PLAYS

The Silver Tassie

The Silver Tassie: A Tragi-Comedy in Four Acts was produced at the Apollo Theatre, in London, in 1929. The play represents O'Casey's first break with the traditional realism of his first three, very successful plays. The plot centers on a fabulous young athlete who becomes an infantry soldier during World War I and is left permanently crippled by an enemy attack. The title of the play is taken from the Scottish ballad by Robert Burns entitled "The Silver Tassie." (The word *tassie* means *cup*.) The song describes the departure of a reluctant soldier from his "bonnie lassie" as he prepares to board ship for the battle ground. O'Casey introduced the ballad at the end of the first act during a similar situation.

In the first act, we are introduced to Harry Heegan, the fabulous local athlete, who has won a cup (the Silver Tassie) for his football club and is now returning, reluctantly, to the trenches. We also meet: Harry's sensual and adoring girl friend, Jessie Taite; his parents, Mr. and Mrs. Sylvester Heegan, and his parents' friend Simon Norton—all of whom adulate Harry; Susie Monican, who, thwarted in love for Harry, has turned to evangelical Christianity; the upstairs neighbor Teddy Foran, a soldier who bullies his wife; and Barney Bagnal, also a soldier who venerates the heroic athlete Harry.

The second act, which is a symbolic commentary on war and does not contribute to the dramatic action in the usual sense, will be discussed below.

The third act is set in a hospital, after the war: Teddy Foran is blind; Harry is a cripple in a wheelchair; Jessie has deserted Harry for Barney, now a war hero; and the formerly religious Susie, now a nurse, loves a doctor on the hospital staff. Tormented by the loss of Jessie and his crippled condition, Harry alternates between hysterical outbursts of anger and calm prayer for the success of a forthcoming operation that may heal him.

The last act shows the football-club dance with an amorous Jessie in the arms of a lascivious Barney. His operation having been a failure, Harry pursues the couple in his wheelchair, hurling insults that finally provoke Jessie's new lover to attack him physically. Unable to bear exclusion from the world of ordinary men, Harry crushes and tosses aside the Silver Tassie, the trophy he described in earlier, happier times as a sign of youth, sign of strength, sign of victory." The cup thus comes to symbolize the life in death to which Harry and Teddy have been consigned by their unfortunate fate in the war and by their former friends and admirers, who have utterly forsaken them.

The first, third, and last acts become increasingly unrealistic as the story of young Harry and his fellow soldier Teddy unfolds. The first act is typically realistic until, at the end, the departing soldiers and the farewell crowd begin a wild chanting. The third act in the hospital ward, with Harry's emotional outbursts, has an atmosphere of controlled violence bordering on insanity; the overall effect is one of semirealism. The fourth act gives the initial impression of realism but very quickly changes into an expressionistic nightmare as the chanted, biblically inspired laments of the maimed Harry and Teddy are heard against the frivolous chatter and sensuous music of the dance.

O'Casey's most original technique for conveying his theme of the terrible sufferings—spiritual and physical —of the common soldier in wartime occurs in the totally expressionistic treatment of setting, character, and language in the symbolic second act. Although there are many variations in expressionistic methods, the technique usually employs abrupt or staccato dialogue, symbolic rather than realistic characters, choral or mass groups, and the use of lighting and color for unrealistic effects. O'Casey utilized these methods in what was, for him, a departure from his earlier use of traditional forms of dramaturgy.

Act II takes place in a military installation somewhere in France. The scene is a jagged, lacerated ruin of what was once a monastery, "a little distorted from its original appearance," according to the stage directions. At the back of the stage, the destroyed wall and window of the monastery are indicated by broken roof coping. Its jagged right wall, part of which remains intact, holds a stained glass window showing a figure of the Virgin Mary. Further up from the window is a life-size crucifix damaged by shells.

In the center of the back wall, where the arch of the monastery should be, stands a big, black howitzer with its squat, heavy undercarriage and barrel angled toward the front stage. Shattered tree stumps and shell holes disfigure the landscape beyond the howitzer; forms that look like the hands of a corpse protrude from rubbish heaps; in the red glare of the distant horizon, one can see crisscrossed barbed wire; a green star and a white star alternately burn in the heavens.

Groups of soldiers huddled onstage are symbolic rather than individualized characters. Crouching above them, on a ramp over to one side of the stage, is a half-crazed soldier (The Croucher) whose clothes are covered with blood and mud. The Croucher's head looks like a skull and his hands like those of a skeleton.

When the act begins, rain is falling and cries of wounded men can be heard. The sound of a small organ from behind the fragmented monastery wall accompanies the monks' celebration of the Mass. At the same time, The Croucher intones a kind of litany; the incantation of the *Kyrie eleison* (the formalized plea to God for mercy) is heard periodically when he pauses.

As The Croucher ends his litany prophesying death and destruction to all, an exhausted party of soldiers shuffles onstage, joining those already huddled under the ramp. They begin to chant in free-verse, staccato phrases, as if in response to The Croucher's litany. The form is reminiscent of Gregorian chant. The soldiers are deeply bitter about the war's disruptive effect upon their lives, but they reject The Croucher's prophecy of death and stress their belief in a benificent God and in the war weaponry that may save them from the enemy.

An army official comes onstage with the news that the enemy has broken through their lines. The soldiers hurry into position by the howitzer, which swings around and points away from the audience to the distant horizon. As a shell is swung into the breech by the soldiers, a flash indicates the firing of the gun. At the same time, searchlights begin to move over the sky. There is no sound whatsoever. The stage darkens slowly, but distant flashes occasionally light up the scene. The soldiers continue to load and fire the howitzer with rhythmic, robotlike movements. The curtain descends.

O'Casey considered *The Silver Tassie* his best play by far at the time he wrote it in 1928. He sent the completed manuscript to the Abbey Theatre, so certain the company would produce it that he subsequently sent a letter suggesting various actors for the characters. However, he received the following letter from Yeats (published in *The Letters of Sean O'Casey*), who wrote for the board of directors of the Abbey:

> I had looked forward with great hope and excitement to reading your play. . . . I am sad and discouraged; you have no subject. You were interested in the Irish Civil War . . .
>
> But you are not interested in the great war; you never stood on its battlefields or walked its hospitals, and so write out of your own opinions. You illustrated those opinions by a series of almost unrelated scenes. . . . there is no dominating character, no dominating action, neither psychological unity nor unity of action. . . .
>
> This is a hateful letter to write. . . .
>
> W. B. Yeats
> 20 April 1928

The reaction of Yeats to the play was a bitter disappointment to O'Casey. He wrote a stinging rebuttal in which he accused Yeats of being interested in experimental forms only so long as they reflected his theatrical preferences. One heartening communication did come from his great friend and mentor, G. B. Shaw, who wrote him enthusiastically that it was "a hell of a play" and hailed O'Casey as a "Titan."

After many difficulties in mounting its unusual second act, *The Silver Tassie* finally opened at the Apollo Theater in London, on 12 October 1929. The producer, C. B. Cochran, engaged the Canadian-born Raymond Massey as director. Augustus John, the famous painter and a personal friend of O'Casey's, designed the set for the second act. Charles Laughton was cast as

Harry Heegan and Barry Fitzgerald as Sylvester Heegan, his father.

Everyone involved in the production was wrought up on opening night. Many problems developed—for one, the overpowering set of John (who had had no previous stage experience) was so heavy that the stage hands could barely move it about. Nonetheless, the audience reaction was tremendous, and the critical reviews that appeared were favorable for the most part.

In September 1949, the Interplayers staged *The Silver Tassie* at Carnegie Hall in New York City. (The play had been seen in New York only once before in a minor, apparently unauthorized, production, at the Greenwich Village Theater.) According to Brooks Atkinson (in the *New York Times*, 4 September 1949), the Interplayers lacked individual abilities but the direction of Al Saxe wielded the group into a coherent production. Jack Palance was particularly effective in the role of Harry Heegan. And Atkinson felt that the Interplayers had done a signal service in bringing the play to the boards.

Within the Gates

Published in 1933, *Within the Gates* had its premiere at the Royalty Theatre, London, in 1934. The play, O'Casey's first full-length treatment in the expressionistic style, is set within the gates of a park similar to London's Hyde Park during the great depression of the 1930s. The dramatic action takes place in four scenes: a spring morning; a summer noon; an autumn evening; and a winter night. The characters are representative types rather than individualized persons.

The main plot centers on the struggle among the various characters for the soul of The Young Woman, Jannice, who is dying of a heart condition. The Dreamer (a poet), The Atheist, The Bishop, and The Salvation Army Officer try to persuade Jannice to accept what each believes to be the means of salvation. Although she dies making the sign of the cross, it is The Dreamer's humanistic vision of salvation that Jannice ultimately embraces.

O'Casey's central thrust in *Within the Gates* is that bourgeois capitalism and institutionalized Christianity have caused both economic and spiritual depression in western society by repressing rather than celebrating life. O'Casey indicated through Jannice's experiences that salvation cannot be found in the trite sloganeering offered by state and church but must be found in a humanistic vision of life that encompasses youth, joy, love, and art, as well as economic security and political freedom—a vision expressed by the poet-Dreamer.

Within the Gates—O'Casey's "cry for humanity"—has often been described as a modern morality play. The struggle for Jannice's soul by characters who represent good or evil parallels the dramatic action in the Dutch morality play *Everyman* (1495). The allegorical Everyman journeys to his grave tempted by good and bad acquaintances and encouraged by the ministrations of heaven. Symbolically, the dying Jannice also stands for every man and woman in search of salvation in a trying world. Her aid and comfort is the poet-Dreamer, who is a symbol of the creative spirit of God, the Holy Ghost, according to O'Casey, which "first rises out of the ruck of things" and establishes beauty and order. (Letter to the *Evening Standard* of London, 9 December 1933.)

O'Casey constructed the play in the expressionistic style of the later Strindberg, Ernst Toller, and Eugene O'Neill, a style basically of distortion and simplicity. He employed an unreal atmosphere and quality of action; color, lighting, and geometrical forms to give the stage settings an antirealistic quality; and choral or mass groups, as well as representative types, rather than realistic characters. His objective was an interpretation of humanity in its spiritual aspect: his goal, amelioration of the human condition.

Within the Gates was revolutionary for its time both in form and theme. After reading the published play, Eugene O'Neill sent O'Casey (in a letter of 15 December 1933) his "enthusiastic congratulations" for "a splendid piece of work." He went on to say that he was especially moved and "greenly envious" of its "rare and sensitive poetic beauty." And he thanked O'Casey for having mentioned in his preface to the play that he had been inspired by O'Neill's *Mourning Becomes Electra.*

Presented at London's Royalty Theatre in February 1934, the play ran only a few weeks to generally unfavorable reviews. Nevertheless, it was bought by an American impresario for production in New York and opened at the National Theater there on 22 October 1934, with Lillian Gish as Jannice and Bramwell Fletcher as The Dreamer. Most American critics were highly enthusiastic and a tour of twelve cities was planned. But the tour was interrupted before it really began when several church organizations fought successfully to ban the play in Boston.

The Star Turns Red

O'Casey wrote *The Star Turns Red* for an amateur group connected with the left-wing Unity Theatre in London, where it was first performed in March 1940. It is a play of ideas depicting the conflict between communism and fascism. The communists are represented by the oppressed workers, the Red Guards (a militant group of workers), and their heroic leader Red Jim; the fascists, by the Saffron Shirts (modeled on the storm troops of the Nazi regime), the Purple Priest, and the Catholic Christian Front, which controls the government, the labor unions, and the church. In the course of the dramatic action, the rebelling workers overthrow the government and establish a dictatorship of the proletariat.

The first of four acts is set in the Dublin home of the Old Man, the Old Woman, and their sons, Jack and Kian, during the last hours of a Christmas Eve sometime in the future. The silhouettes of two factory chimneys are visible through the left rear window; the outline of a church spire, a silver star nearby (symbolizing the Star of Bethlehem), is discernible through the right rear window. Beneath the left window is a

161

sketch of Lenin and beneath the right one, a sketch of a bishop's mitered head.

There are several brief episodes in the act. The militant young communist Jack defends Red Jim in a bitter argument with his brother Kian, who is a member of the Saffron Shirts. The Lord Mayor discloses that the Trades Congress union has voted to oust Red Jim from the Central Council in order to restrict his influence among the rank-and-file workers. A group of Saffron Shirts threatens Jack, demanding he abjure communism. When Jack's girl friend, Julia, tries to interfere, the leader of the Saffron Shirts has her whipped by his followers. Michael, Julia's father and a disciple of Red Jim, tries to strike the leader, but he is shot fatally by Kian.

Act II takes place at the headquarters of the General Workers' Union. The church spire has receded farther into the background and the factory chimneys seem to be closer and larger than in the previous act. A black poster with a red hammer and sickle sketched on a white cross has replaced the pictures of Lenin and the bishop. A banner reads: "An Injury to One Is the Concern of All."

Caheer, Brallain, Eglish, Sheasker, and the Secretary are all depicted by O'Casey as unscrupulous union executives, in reality enemies of the working class whose interests they presumably represent. Red Jim, patterned after the Irish labor leader James Larkin, is a fearless labor organizer who defies the union officials to vote him out of the Central Council. The act ends with the Red Guards holding the union officials captive in headquarters.

The setting in Act III is similar to that of Act I except that Michael's body rests on a bier under the right window. A black pall with a crucifix covers the body, and a red banner, emblazoned by a hammer and sickle, hangs over the dead man's face.

Maimed and sick neighbors, representative of the Christian poor, come in to view the body and revile the world of communism described to them by a hostile clergy. Jack and four of Red Jim's followers come in to carry the body to its final resting place. But they are hindered by the Purple Priest and several confraternity men, who also try to claim the body. Red Jim enters and denounces the Purple Priest for his indifference to the poor. The act ends with Red Jim and his followers carrying the coffin of Michael off the stage; they march to the rhythm of a communist song.

The events of Act IV take place in the Lord Mayor's residence, where a Christmas party is to be held. The factory chimneys now loom larger through the left window. And the star that shone beside the church spire now shines beside the chimneys.

During this act, the workers' revolution, sparked by a police attempt to arrest Red Jim, begins. The music of the Internationale, the sounds of galloping horses, gunfire, and sirens are heard in the streets. In the midst of the uproar the star turns red, a symbolic indication of victory for the workers. Red Guards, followed by Red Jim, enter and begin to sandbag the windows. The curtain is lowered to represent the passing of several hours. In the brief denouement that follows, Red Jim is told that Jack has been killed in the fighting and that the soldiers have joined the workers. The curtain falls as the red star seems to grow bigger and the workers chant the Internationale.

O'Casey, in a letter to Ronald G. Rollins (25 July 1959), said of *The Star Turns Red* that it was a play of political prophecy, based on the views of James Larkin and written in the language and protests of the Bible. The play was condemned by most critics as pure propaganda, totally without dramatic merit. G. B. Shaw disagreed. In a postcard to O'Casey (22 April 1940), he commented: "It shewed up the illiteracy of the critics, who didn't know that like a good Protestant you had brought the language of the Authorized Version [of the Bible] back to life. Splendid!"

Oak Leaves and Lavender

Published in 1946, *Oak Leaves and Lavender* was produced in 1947 at the Lyric Theatre in
London. The dramatic action of the play takes place in
Cornwall during World War II when German bombers raided London daily in the Battle of Britain. A
Prelude is followed by three acts; the play ends with
what might be called an epilogue, although O'Casey
did not indicate a formal division. All of the scenes are
set in the great room of a manor owned by the wealthy,
aging Dame Hatherleigh.

The Hatherleigh manor is serving as headquarters
for various civilian organizations devoted to the war
effort. Feelim O'Morrigun, the Irish butler, is in charge
of the wartime operations. His son Drishogue and the
Dame's son Edgar are Royal Air Force cadets.

In the Prelude, the ghosts of elegant aristocrats
dressed in silks and satins dance a slow minuet as they
lament that the values of their society are no longer
sufficient to England's needs. As a Young Girl walks
among the dancers selling lavender, the Young Son of
Time warns that England is in imminent danger. The
masquelike, unreal quality of the Prelude changes into

a realistic atmosphere in Act I, but the scent of lavender, noted by several characters, remains.

In the course of the action, Edgar and Drishogue are killed in an air battle with the invading German bombers. Drishogue, a dedicated communist, had justified his participation in the war by stating he was not fighting for capitalist England but for "the people," in the name of those communists who died at Guernica during the Spanish Civil War.

In the epilogue ending the play, Dame Hatherleigh joins the figures of the dancing ghosts who appeared earlier in the Prelude. She comments sadly that her generation is at an end, but "Our end makes but a beginning for the others." One of the gentleman dancers adds: "The lavender will bloom again, and oak leaves laugh at the wind in the storm."

The title *Oak Leaves and Lavender, or a Warld [World] on Wallpaper* is explained in part by the above quotations. The lavender, a symbol of the death of aristocracy and privilege, will bloom again in the sense that certain worthwhile traditions will stand the test of the hour. The lavender will bloom next to the oak leaves, which represent the sturdy forces that "will laugh at the wind in the storm" of fascism as they create a new world.

The subtitle is an ironic reference to Yeats's criticism, in 1928, of O'Casey's *Silver Tassie*. Yeats had written to O'Casey that the war (in that play, World War I) obtruded itself too much into the dramatic action; it should have been reduced to "wallpaper in front of which the characters must pose and speak." O'Casey rejected his advice. In *Oak Leaves and Lavender*, he again used world conflict as an "obtrusive" force in the dramatic action. And, instead of reducing it to "wallpaper," he symbolically magnified the conflict by transforming the great room of the Hatherleigh manor into a war factory.

In form, *Oak Leaves and Lavender* is an expression-istic play that utilizes unrealistic narrative elements, symbolic devices of light and sound, and emblematic settings. The aristocratic ghosts from the past are nar-rators who also comment on the theme of the play. When the two air-force cadets are preparing to leave for their stations in London, unseen trumpets sound the first line of *Deutschland über Alles*, a threatening voice proclaims "Germany calling," an air-raid warn-ing wails, the music of "The Ride of the Valkyries" gets louder, several tongues of flame shoot into the air, and a crowd spontaneously chants encouragement to the departing flyers.

The wartime changes in England are represented by increasingly expressionistic distortion in the appear-ance of the great room of the manor. In the Prelude the three chandeliers' resemblance to giant gantries is merely suggested; by Act III, it is obvious. In that act the emblematic transformation of the setting is com-plete: the paneling of the room has become like ties, belts, and bars connecting various parts of machinery; the fireplace has assumed the shape of a great drop forge; the bureau looks like a lathe; and two small windows seem to be wheels carrying belts up to the chandelier-gantries. When a young foreman blows a whistle at the end of the act, the room becomes alive with belts that move, wheels that turn, and the drop forge that rises and falls. The clanking of steel is ac-companied by sounds indicating the orderly bustle of a factory.

Oak Leaves and Lavender is a prophecy of victory for the Allied cause over the Axis powers; of victory for communism over fascism. Even though O'Casey was on the side of the angels, the play was never popular in England: Drishogue was too vociferous a communist for the taste of most spectators; and the expressionistic settings posed technical problems for the designer that were difficult to solve.

In *Sean*, Mrs. O'Casey spoke of the London premiere of the play as a miserable experience for the entire family. She thought the play was so poorly directed that it was only a ghost of the original script.

The Bishop's Bonfire

The Bishop's Bonfire: A Sad Play within the Tune of a Polka had its premiere in Dublin, at the Gaiety Theatre, on 28 February 1955. The play—its time, "the present"—concerns the elaborate preparations in the Irish village Ballyoonagh for the visit of the Roman Catholic Bishop and native son Bill Mullarky. The village's wealthiest citizen and largest landowner, Councillor Reiligan, who has just been made a papal count, and the parish priest, the Very Reverend Timothy Canon Burren, are in charge of the festivities, which include the igniting of a great bonfire of books and pictures considered immoral.

The Reiligan family includes a son Michael, a lieutenant home on leave, and two daughters, Keelin and Foorawn. Keelin is in love with the laborer Daniel Clooncoohy, a match opposed by her father on the basis of class and money. Foorawn has taken a vow of chastity but is still in love with Manus Moanroe, who left the priesthood because of love for her. Father Boheroe, a curate who combines a religious mysticism with a love for "the beautiful flesh of humanity," tries to encourage the sisters and their lovers, but he is strongly opposed by Canon Burren, a close ally of Councillor Reiligan.

Several workmen, Daniel, Codger Sleehaun, the Prodical, and Rankin, are refurbishing the Reiligan house for Bishop Mullarky's visit. Codger Sleehaun is a merry, wise, compassionate old farm hand—one of the best although close to ninety—who is still sensitive to the beauty in nature and the joys of life. The Prodical, a mason, is an intemperate, caustic Protestant who loves nothing better than to do battle with Rankin, a puritanical, ill-natured Catholic.

The workmen, says Councillor Reiligan, "demonstrate destruction" instead of refurbishing the house. In the midst of drinking and arguing, they spill cement on a new rug, throw around expensive furniture, and destroy an exotic plant. Whenever the men make a blasphemous comment or try to hide their gin keg, however, a religious statue they call "the buckineeno boyo" gives out a blast on its trumpet. (The statue represents a martyred Roman legionary—the special saint of the Bishop—noted for the miraculous power of its horn.)

In the midst of these lively, duple-meter antics, the sad story of Reiligan's daughters is played out. Despite her wishes, Keelin is engaged to a wealthy old farmer who is a brother of the Bishop. She finally breaks with Daniel because he, frightened by the opposition of Councillor Reiligan and Canon Burren, refuses to leave Ireland with her. Foorawn, despite her own tortured feelings, prepares to enter a convent. Having decided to leave the village, the embittered Manus tries to steal money collected by Foorawn for the church. She apprehends him, they quarrel, and he shoots her. In the throes of death, Foorawn writes a letter absolving Manus of all guilt by pretending suicide. After she admits her love for him and dies, Manus reads the letter aloud:

"I can bear this life no longer. Good-bye all. Foo-rawn." (*He slowly places the paper back on the table.*) Oh, my poor Foorawn! My sombre musk rose: my withered musk rose now!

He is described by O'Casey as "slouching away out of sight."

Most of the sympathetic characters also leave the village. The Codger is banned from the village by Canon Burren because he points out that the country-side owned by Reiligan is blighted, unfruitful—"no heart in the soil, no heart in the grass that tops it." In a confrontation with Reiligan, the Codger accuses him of owning the land, the tavern, the shirt factory, the dance hall, even the people—and of being a regular menace. The Codger bitterly decries the alliance of church and state seen in the conniving of Councillor Reiligan and Canon Burren. With the departure of the Codger, Father Boheroe, who tried to defend him, also leaves the village. The bonfire is ignited at the end of the play.

In a program note written for the premiere perfor-mance, O'Casey said he was trying to tell the story of "a land where chastity has become one of the worst vices, the marriage rate the lowest in the world and the birthrate too." He added that the play is also meant to show a mixture of "piety and profits, venomous puritanism and the ignorance of all around."

The play's subtitle, "A Sad Play within the Tune of a Polka," reflects the double plot of the unfortunate Reiligan daughters and the lively workmen, the one melodramatic and the other farcical in tone. Although both plots end in pathos, the grim shooting of Foo-rawn seems dissonant in tone to the joyous bickering of the workmen.

Ultimately, repression, pietism, commercialism, and philistinism win over freedom, joy, love, and beauty.

The controlling symbolism employed by O'Casey is that of sterility—sterility of the land and in the people, caused in great part by a reactionary state and church working hand in glove.

Before the opening of Cyril Cusak's production in Dublin, in 1955, the Dublin newspaper the *Standard* helped to create a climate of hostility toward O'Casey by damning him as anti-Catholic and his play as dangerous. No serious rioting, however, occurred on opening night, even though many people jammed the area around the theater. Tyrone Guthrie, who directed the play, relates an amusing incident of the evening in his book *A Life in the Theatre* (1959).

According to him, the most vociferous voices among the crowd outside the theater were those of Catholic students from National University demonstrating against O'Casey and those of Protestant students from Trinity College demonstrating for him. Finally, the mounted police were called in to disperse the noisy crowd, but the Protestants would not give up the field. A fatherly old policeman left to guard the doors was faced with the chanting students who were disturbing the audience inside:

> "Listen," he said to the Trinity boys. "Are youse fellers for O'Casey?"
> "We are. *We want O'Casey!*"
> "Well then for Jesus' sake will ye f—— off and let them that have paid for it hear what your man wrote."
> And straightway they f——ed off. . . .

Virtually all the Irish critics were bitterly hostile to play and playwright. Their argument was that O'Casey had been living abroad so long that he had no true picture of life in Ireland.

In a vitriolic article entitled "Bonfire under a Black

Sun" (in *The Green Crow*) O'Casey answered their accusations, one by one, by citing facts that had appeared in Irish newspapers and journals, which, he felt, substantiated his view that Ireland—to its detriment—was dominated by the clergy in every aspect of life whether political, social, intellectual, or artistic. O'Casey ended his article by saying, "No hope then for Ireland? A lot of it, for hope springs infernal in the Irish breast," his own included.

The Drums of Father Ned

The Drums of Father Ned, or A Mickrocosm of Ireland was first produced in 1959 in Lafayette, Indiana. Comprised of a "Prerumble" and three acts, the play is set in the Irish town of Doonavale. The plot is about the preparations being made by the young people of the town for the Tostal, a spring festival devoted to the arts of the past and of the present.

In the "Prerumble," which takes place shortly before the Irish Civil War, English soldiers are burning the town of Doonavale. In the midst of the flaming background, only a church spire and a tottering Celtic cross can be seen. The soldiers are teasing Binnington and McGilligan, who were once close friends. They grew up together, fought the English, and married sisters. But they are now mortal enemies because Binnington is a Free Stater and McGilligan, a Republican.

The English soldiers force them to speak and argue with one another by shooting bullets over their heads when they refuse to cooperate. One soldier offers not to burn the town's round tower, a symbol of the Celtic past, if the men will reconcile their differences, but they savagely refuse. A strange Echo repeats their angry words in a mocking tone.

The scene then shifts to the present. Binnington—now the mayor of Doonavale, as well as a solicitor and owner of the general store—and McGilligan—now deputy mayor and building contractor—are still mortal enemies, but they make financial deals because, as they often say, "Business is business"—words repeated in a mocking tone by the Echo.

Binnington and McGilligan, with the hearty endorsement of Father Fillifogue, object that the young people of the town are much too involved in the Tostal planning of decorations, pageants, and recitals of classical music. They should be attending to business and showing more piety and restraint. (The Echo repeats their protests, mockingly.) Two of the ringleaders of the young people are Michael, Binnington's son, and Nora, McGilligan's daughter. Much against their fathers' wishes, they are also lovers.

Michael and Nora argue that Father Ned, the priest who goes about the countryside rehearsing for the procession that will initiate the Tostal, has taught them that God manifests Himself in many ways other than in piety and restraint. God also manifests Himself in the arts, in the shout of joy in a street, even in the love between two young people. Not only is Father Ned the spirit behind the Tostal, he is also behind the reorganization of the town's library committee, formerly dominated by Father Fillifogue who considered almost all books dangerous to morality. At the end of the play, Michael and Nora announce that they plan to marry despite parental opposition and that they also intend to run for the offices of mayor and deputy mayor.

The young couple and the other young people of Doonavale represent for O'Casey the hope of Ireland. They have rid themselves of the stultifying, embittered influence of Binnington, McGilligan, and Father Fillifogue for a new concept of life in Doonavale.

Father Ned, the Echo, and Angus the Young (a Celtic deity represented on a shield to be used in the Tostal procession) symbolize that new concept of a life, which encompasses the arts, beauty, love, and the Celtic past. Father Ned is never seen on stage, but the drumming heard from offstage is associated with him. The Echo frequently mocks the words of businessmen who are opposed to the spirit of Father Ned. Angus the Young was the Celtic god of youth, art, love, and enlightenment; the values for which he stood are the same as those of Father Ned.

Although Robert Hogan's 1959 production mounted at the Little Theater in Indiana was the premiere of the play, it was not meant to be originally. Sometime in 1957, O'Casey had been asked to submit a play for the Dublin Tostal. He consented and sent *The Drums of Father Ned*. But the Archbishop of Dublin refused to open the celebration with a mass if the O'Casey play (as well as one by Joyce) were included. After much fruitless letter writing, O'Casey withdrew his play and angrily banned all productions of his work in Ireland.

AN EVALUATION OF
THE DRAMATIST

Early in O'Casey's career, Lady Gregory wrote him: "I believe there is something in you and your strong point is characterization" (quoted in *Lady Gregory's Journals*). As she recognized, his natural talent lay in characterization through language, and he learned to write dialogue capable of mirroring very diverse types. The following speeches have been selected to give the reader some indication of the range in O'Casey's cast of loquacious characters. For the purpose of this limited discussion, the character types selected might be described as the "bravura" Irishman, the prophet, the romantic young militant, and the vaudeville team.

The dialogue of the bravura Irishman is often characterized by malapropisms, redundancies, polysyllabic neologisms, and fractured Latin. He tends to be circumlocutory rather than direct and unconsciously employs a kind of mock logic. In the following quotation from *Cock-a-doodle Dandy*, the puritanical ignoramus Shanaar is counseling the equally unpleasant old Michael Marthraun on how to control a servant girl and how to cleanse the house of a giant cock—presumably an evil spirit—that has invaded it.

> I'd recommend you to compel her, for a start, to lift her bodice higher up, an' pull her skirt lower

down; for th' circumnambulatory nature of a woman's form often has a detonatin' effect on a man's
idle thoughts. . . . Mr. Marthraun, don't forget to
have th' room, where th' commotion was mani-
fested, *turbulenta concursio cockolorum*, purified
an' surified be an understandin' clergyman. Good-
bye. Be on your guard against any unfamiliar motion or peculiar conspicuosity or quasimodical
addendum, perceivable in any familiar thing or
creature common to your general recognisances.
A cat barkin' at a dog, or a dog miaouin' be a fire
would atthract your attention, give you a shock,
but don't for th' love of God, notice it! It's this
scourge of materialism sweepin' th' world, that's
incantatin' these evils to our senses and our door-
steps. . . . An' th' coruscatin' conduct in th' dance-
halls is completin' th' ruin.

The dialogue of the character who might be described as the prophet is very different in sound and
sense from the bravura Irishman just quoted. The
prophet's speech is often based on evenly balanced
phrases and clauses (parison) in parallel formation.
The parisonic exactness is emphasized by arrangement
of the sentences in climactic order. This type of speech
is usually constructed on the periodic sentence, in
which the effect of suspense is heightened by the rep-
etition of a word or words at the beginning of succes-
sive sentences (anaphora). Often the words echo biblical phraseology. The psychological effect upon the
listener of such ordered, rhetorical speech is that of
incantation or ritual. In the following quotation from
The Star Turns Red, the union organizer Red Jim is
addressing the reactionary Purple Priest, who is trying
to prevent a workers' strike by demanding absolute
obedience to the authority of the church, which he
claims to represent.

If the heritage of heaven be the heritage here of shame and rags and the dead puzzle of poverty, then we turn our backs on it! If your God stands for one child to be born in a hovel and another in a palace, then we declare against him. If your God declares that one child shall be clad in silks and another in sores, then we declare against him. If your God declares that it takes a sack of sovereigns to keep one child and a handful of pence to keep another, then we declare against him. If your God declares that one child shall dwell in the glory of knowledge and another shall die in the poverty of ignorance, then we declare against him: once and for all and for ever we declare against your God, who hath filled the wealthy with good things and hath sent the poor empty away!

There is another type of O'Casey hero, usually younger than the prophet, who is a romantic, left-wing militant. Underlying his dialogue is an elaborate logical structure based on the artful balance of similar elements within the same sentence, or among several sentences. Many of the lines, freighted with elaborate images of nature and loving epithets, are highly alliterated and cadenced. In the following quotation from *Purple Dust*, O'Killigain, a communist veteran of the Spanish Civil War, is trying to persuade lovely young Avril to leave her financial provider in his decrepit mansion and accompany him to the mountains, back to nature where true love can flourish:

An' you, young girl, sweet bud of an out-spreading three [tree], graft yourself on to the living, and don't stay hidden any longer here. Come where the rain is heavy, where the frost frets, and where the sun is warm. Avril, pulse of me heart, listen to me, an' let longin' flood into your heart for the call of life. The young thorn-three withered away now,

can awaken again, an' spread its fragrance around
us. Spit out what's here, an' come where love is
fierce an' fond an' fruitful. Come, lass, where
there's things to say an' things to do an' love at the
endings!

O'Casey was equally capable of writing dialogue for
an old married couple, highly argumentative and iras-
cible with one another. Their lines sound like the
music-hall turn typical of a vaudeville team. In the
following quotation from the one-act play *Figuro in
the Night*, the Old Man and his wife have somehow
moved in their conversation from a garden to God to
Adam and Eve.

> OLD MAN: A garden is a lovesome thing, God wot,
> and that was God's own garden, woman.
> OLD WOMAN: God's wot what?
> OLD MAN: What God's what's what?
> OLD WOMAN: I'm asking you what's God's whot?
> OLD MAN: How can I tell what's God's whot's
> wot? It's what's not your what's whot or my
> wot's what. Only God wots what His own wot is.
> OLD WOMAN: You're thinking so high that you
> don't know even what's your own whot's wot, or
> mine, or even Adam and Eve's, who well knew
> what was whot when she wove thread from a
> lamb's fleece into strips that Adam colored a rich
> blue from the juice of an herb growing among
> the radishes, using the strips to brighten the
> lustre of her bonnie brown hair.

These diverse examples of O'Casey's dialogue only
begin to give the reader some indication of how finely
he had honed his talent for characterization through
language.

If we were to try to describe O'Casey's dramatic
writing in general, one might say it is distinguished by

melodious epithets, extended metaphors, and recondite symbols; by exclamatory statements, rhetorical questions, and inverted word order; by puns, limericks, and songs; by political, historical, and mythological allusions; by catalogs, linguistic fancies, and mock logic; by Gaelic overtones, biblical phraseology, and fractured Latin; by straightaway statement and oblique remark.

O'Casey's mastery was not confined to his use of language, however; his control and innovation in dramatic form was also impressive. From the beginning of his career, O'Casey employed certain techniques such as multiple plots, detailed stage directions, antiheroic irony and antirealistic symbolism, the mingling of realistic, fantastic, and poetic modes, the fusion of the tragic with the comic temper, the use of melodrama, satire, burlesque, and farce, the concentration on theatricality in settings, the incorporation of music and dance. And he utilized these techniques within the concept of drama as a parable that is both entertainment and an illustration of the conflict between man's will and society's strictures. Although O'Casey was very often criticized for having broken with his earlier realism (of, for example, *Juno and the Paycock*) for totally different forms such as expressionism (*Within the Gates*) or fantasy (*Cock-a-doodle Dandy*), no such dramatic break ever occurred—the emphasis changed.

In addition to the full-length plays mentioned, O'Casey wrote several shorter dramas listed in the chronology. Many of them are delightful little pieces, also innovative in form, with gems of characterization and splendid dialogue.

O'Casey had his share of hostile criticism. The highly controversial nature of his ideas and his combative personality made him a target of critics ranging from arrogant to absurd. He was often advised, ill-naturedly, to go back to Ireland where he belonged; to give up his foolish experimentation and return to the tried-and-true formula of his early plays; to renounce communism for the superior virtues found in bourgeois capitalism and Christianity. He was even advised to give up writing altogether, for he was nothing more —some critics said—than a meagerly talented, blasphemous upstart with a penchant for the obscene.

More sympathetic critics, embarrassed by his left-wing radicalism, sometimes unconsciously patronized O'Casey by intimating that underneath his argumentative and outrageous talk was really a good fellow whose political ideas were not to be taken seriously. These critics disgusted O'Casey as much as those who dared advise him directly on matters pertaining to his personal and artistic beliefs.

No one, however, can deny O'Casey's deep commitment to the ideals of energy, youth, faith, beauty, joy, and art. His habitual patterns of feeling might be described as sentimental, lyric, rhapsodic, comic, ironic, and even bitter. He was a secular humanist who demanded a decent life for every human being on earth, and defeat for those who would deny man that heritage. O'Casey saw the world as it is, and he projected the world as he felt it could be.

For some forty years O'Casey worked diligently, and happily, to attain the dramatic goal he articulated in "The Play of Ideas" in 1950 (in *Blasts and Benedictions*). It was to join the variety, richness, and daring of the great tradition in drama to the republican ideals of the common man:

> The plays written around the new life must be currents in the mainstream of drama, must be an offspring of the great tradition. When we decide, instead of playing at being kings or queens or cavaliers, to play at being proletarians, then let us

play at being them, and not send them forth as lecturers in an academy hall, preachers in a pulpit or speakers from a political platform, important as these activities can be. The dramatist must see poetry in the smoky hub-bub of a tavern, just as he may see it in the stately ceremonial of a cathedral, though he may realize that, while the life in a tavern is always real, that of the cathedral is often a sham. . . .

I look forward to the day with confidence when British workers will carry in their hip pockets a volume of Keats' poems or a Shakespeare play beside the packets of lunch attached to their belts.

EPILOGUE:
A TALE OF TWO IRELANDS

> I know the mind of Ireland because I am within it; I
> know the heart of Ireland because I am one of its
> corners; I know the five senses of Ireland because I
> am within them and they are within me; they bid me
> look, and when I look, I see; they bid me listen, and
> when I listen, I hear.
>
> Sean O'Casey: "Bonfire under a
> Black Sun," in *The Green Crow*

Ireland, inhabited by a Celtic people since about
350 B.C., was a country of clans governed by chiefs
who engaged in frequent intertribal warfare. In the
latter half of the twelfth century A.D., one of these
chiefs unwisely enlisted the help of Henry II of England, who willingly sent military aid. Henry's forces
came and conquered for the ambitious chief, but in
1171 Henry himself landed on the island with an army
and proclaimed himself king of the whole of Ireland.

Such was the first in a long series of episodes of
English conquest. For more than five hundred years
following, until the late 1600s, English monarchs pur-
chased the loyalty of the Irish chiefs or waged bloody
war for it. They gained ground and lost it, controlling
now only parts of Ireland, now the entire island. But
they always managed, more or less, to maintain a
stronghold in the seacoast area around Dublin, an area
later called the Pale. By the 1700s Ireland belonged to
England—or so England thought.

The native Irish fared badly. They were murdered
or driven from their land or allowed to remain only in
exchange for exorbitant taxes to the sovereign. And, by
the time Ireland was firmly in English hands, a reli-

gious persecution that was to continue to plague Ireland to the present day became another of the imperialists' sins. Christianized about the fifth century A.D.—a process attributed in large part to St. Patrick—Ireland recognized the supremacy of the pope during the reign of Henry II in the twelfth century. In the sixteenth century, when Henry VIII broke with the papacy and created a national church separate from the Roman Catholic Church, English influence in Ireland was strong only in the Pale, where Protestantism was accepted and the Church of Ireland established. But foolish imperialistic practices—for example, a policy forbidding the translation of the Book of Common Prayer into Irish—hindered the spread of Protestantism. Beyond the Pale, most of Ireland remained staunchly Roman Catholic.

In 1603, however, Charles Blount, lord deputy of Ireland, transported Irish Catholics from the northern Ulster province and brought in Scottish Presbyterians. This northern province soon became a Protestant enclave. Subsequently, the Puritan Oliver Cromwell, who slaughtered Catholics in his 1649 campaign of conquest and vengeance in Ireland, imposed his policy of "confiscation and plantation," thus saddling the island with a Protestant English landlordry. In the final years of the seventeenth century, during the reign of William and Mary, more landholdings were seized and given over to Protestants from England and Scotland. The Irish Catholics who were allowed to remain on the land and farm it had to pay inordinate rents for this "right," while their landlords lived in England.

By now, a Protestant Anglo-Irish minority had evolved from the imperialists settled on the island. For the most part a moneyed class, they held the power and used it against the natives of the conquered land. In 1691 a code of laws, known as the Penal Code, was developed. In effect until 1778, this system outlawed priests, excluded Catholics from the professions, public office, and parliament, and denied them education, a vote, land, or inheritance. Irish Catholics were reduced to a type of peasant serfdom.

The Protestant Anglo-Irish, however, may have enjoyed the status of preferred citizens—with the help of English laws and arms—but they paid a high price for it. By the late 1700s crippling restrictions on Irish trade, the source of much of their income, and its subjection to English interests had angered the Anglo-Irish minority. The Irish Parliament in Dublin had no real power, for it was still subject to Poynings's Law of 1494, which stipulated that all legislation introduced in Ireland must first be approved by the privy council in England and that all laws passed in England must also apply to Ireland.

While England's attention was temporarily focused on the Revolution in America, a movement was under way to abolish trade restraints and to achieve legislative independence for the Irish Parliament and basic parliamentary reform. Led by Henry Grattan (1746–1820), a member of the Irish Parliament and a clever strategist, the movement was comprised of members of the Anglo-Irish gentry and middle class and some Catholics. In 1779 the English Parliament gave way under the strong pressure from this group and passed acts (1779, 1780) that lifted many of the restraints on trade. And in 1782 Poynings's Law was repealed. But the issue of parliamentary reform divided the conservatives of the Anglo-Irish establishment from the liberals, themselves divided by the extent of the reforms sought. By 1785 the movement had collapsed.

Continuing forms of repression gave birth to new resistance movements, such as that led by Theobald Wolfe Tone (1763–98), a young Protestant lawyer from Dublin. The objectives of Tone's Society of United Irishmen were wide-ranging: Catholic relief from discriminatory laws; parliamentary and agrarian reform; abolition of compulsory tithes to the church; and representation of both Catholics and Protestants in the national parliament.

Declared illegal and driven underground, the Society of United Irishmen became militant. Their activity inspired the bitter peasants to their own local, armed uprisings. The English retaliated with the Insurrection Act (1796), which resulted in widespread, ferocious repression; the measures taken included home burnings, looting, torture, and murder. This act, coupled with Tone's capture and suicide in 1798, diminished the power behind what threatened to become a national uprising.

In 1801 the English Parliament passed the Act of Union, which formally made Ireland a part of the United Kingdom—that is, England, Scotland, Wales, and Ireland were all now governed by one legislative body. Agitation for repealing this act immediately arose. One movement, led by Daniel O'Connell (1775 –1847), briefly stirred Ireland as no other had with its vast gatherings at rallies. Eventually O'Connell backed down under English pressure, and his movement ended. But Ireland was never to accept this union.

From the efforts of an earlier and more effective movement, also under O'Connell's leadership, had come a pacification measure. In the belief that O'Connell's Catholic Association might bring Ireland to the verge of revolution, the English Parliament passed, in 1829, a bill for Catholic emancipation. Although by this act Catholics were now permitted to be elected to Parliament and to hold public office, property-qualification laws for voting in Ireland were passed at the same time. Nevertheless the act was an important step in the attempt to abolish religious discrimination. The penal laws of 1691 had already been relaxed, and forty years later, another act (1869) would further remove

Catholic disabilities. By the beginning of the twentieth century, a strong Catholic middle class would begin to emerge.

Meanwhile Ireland's economy had made slow progress indeed. The island had been little affected by the rise of industrialism. Although many of the restrictions on Irish trade had been lifted by the English, others remained. There were no tariffs imposed on imports for the protection of existing industries, and many collapsed. In addition, as late as the mid-1800s land laws that were perhaps the most unjust in Europe were still in effect in Ireland. Most of the farming land was owned by absentee landlords and administered by agents. Very often, any guarantee of tenure was refused the tenants, and thus property-improvement initiative was stifled. Having no assurance against sudden eviction and forced to pay incredibly high rents, the peasant farmer was at the mercy of the landlord.

But he was also at the mercy of an indifferent nature. Should his potato crop fail him, he was left without resource. And fail him it often did. The potato blight of 1846 brought one of the most severe famines known to history. During the years 1846–51, an estimated one million starved to death and another million were forced to emigrate, many of them sailing to the United States in the dreaded "coffin ships."

The Irish land question finally became an issue in England. Prime Minister Gladstone (1809–98), aware of the injustice of the land system, managed to pass through Parliament a land act (1870) that guaranteed an evicted tenant compensation for improvements. The act fell far short of remedying the matter, however, for it did not solve the problem of high rents, nor did it insure tenure for the tenant. And payment of compensations by the landlords was easily sidestepped through loopholes in the law. Tenant evictions continued; they even increased and so did armed rebellion.

Out of this national misery had sprung a number of nationalist movements. Perhaps the best known of these was led by the Fenian brotherhood, founded simultaneously in America (by Irish immigrants) and Dublin in 1858. The name of the brotherhood derived from the legendary Fianna, heroic warriors of ancient Ireland. Having Irish independence as their goal, the Fenians were the force behind several violent—but abortive—uprisings. Although the brotherhood dissolved after an unsuccessful rebellion in 1868, their militancy had the long-range effect of dramatizing Ireland's problems. The spirit of the movement itself survived into the early twentieth century through an influential secret society, the Irish Republican Brotherhood. All future Irish nationalists came to be known as Fenians.

Enmeshed with these movements was the Irish Home Rule Party, a political party that sought a moderate form of independence for Ireland. During the late 1870s, this party came under the leadership of the Protestant landowner and aristocrat Charles Steward Parnell (1846–91), a man of charismatic personality. Extraordinarily able and effective, Parnell promoted the cause of Irish home rule by two methods: since the major parties in the House of Commons depended on the votes of his party for a majority, he could extract concessions from them by threatening to obstruct votes; in Ireland, he encouraged agitation to make English rule as difficult as possible and to keep the Irish question before the public. Ireland soon looked to Parnell as its national messiah; the only effect of his incarceration in 1881 for his activities was to further incite the Irish nationalists.

Meanwhile Gladstone persuaded Parliament to pass

a new land act (1881), which granted the so-called three F's—fair rent, fixity of tenure, and free sale by a tenant of his investment in a rented property. But Gladstone's land act came too late. Now intent on complete political independence, Irish leaders continued to agitate against English rule, terrorism grew, and severe repressive measures were taken by Parliament.

Gladstone decided that he must work with Parnell. He brought about his release from prison after Parnell promised to help him pacify Ireland. And he, in turn, promised to assist Parnell in gaining home rule for Ireland. But even more violent outbreaks of Irish terrorism made any concessions impossible, and Gladstone's home-rule bill of 1886 met defeat.

In 1892 Parliament passed a new coercion act, which repressed terrorism temporarily. But perhaps just as damaging to the Irish nationalist spirit was Parnell's involvement in a series of scandals a few years earlier. His downfall was ultimately caused by a highly publicized divorce suit brought against Kitty O'Shea by her husband, who named Parnell as correspondent. The disgrace and death of Ireland's "uncrowned king" in 1891 divided Ireland. Struggles over who would succeed Parnell as leader of the Irish Home Rule Party split the party and drastically reduced its effectiveness. For a time, the Irish cause was greatly weakened in the political arena.

In the early 1890s, a new generation of Irish patriots emerged and began to embark in a different direction —a cultural, literary, and social one. Ireland, they believed, must safeguard its national identity. It must struggle to maintain its imagination and spirituality, to understand, preserve, and develop its cultural heritage. The movement took on an almost evangelical nature as its members proselytized for an Irish Ireland.

Central to the movement was the Gaelic League,

founded in 1893 and led by the Anglo-Irish Protestant Douglas Hyde (1860–1949). (The term *Gaelic* is often used to refer to the language spoken in Ireland and to the remnants of the ancient Celtic culture that survive there.) Hyde's league set out to educate the Irish in Ireland's ancient culture, in its early legends and Celtic mythology. The league sought to preserve Irish as the national language by encouraging all Irishmen to become proficient in reading, writing, and speaking it. (English was the major language in the cities.)

The Gaelic League was presumably nonpolitical, but it helped stoke the fires of nationalism. Padraic Pearse (1879–1916), poet and nationalist, did not exaggerate when he said the Gaelic League "will be recognized in history as the most revolutionary influence that has ever come to Ireland. The Irish Revolution really began when the seven proto-Gaelic Leaguers met in O'Connell Street. . . . The germ of all future Irish history was in that back room."

Simultaneously, the cultural revival was bringing about a golden age in Irish literature, which now began to develop distinctly Irish characteristics. Its writers often drew their themes from mythological or historical characters and stories. Most influential in this cultural movement was the Irish Literary Theater, a society devoted to the development and fostering of a native, poetic drama. Formed in 1899 by William Butler Yeats (1865–1939) and Lady Augusta Gregory (1852–1932), the society was reorganized as the National Theatre Society. From its impetus came the Abbey Theatre in 1904.

The society drew to it the finest talent of the country. Yeats himself, though better remembered as a poet, was probably the first writer of distinctly Irish drama. He wrote and produced for the society several nationalistic verse dramas and the prose drama *Cath-*

leen ní Houlihan, titled after the traditional allegorical name of Ireland, "Cathleen, the daughter of
Houlihan." Lady Gregory, who spoke Irish, tried to
capture the rhythms of peasant speech. She translated
old texts into English and based some of her one-act
plays on them. John Millington Synge (1871–1901),
best known for his *Playboy of the Western World,*
devoted his attention to the peasants of the Aran Is-
lands (off the west coast of Ireland).

In the midst of this flourishing literary activity, a
new kind of struggle was coming to the fore: workers
versus employers. Nowhere in the English-speaking
world were cities so flooded with unskilled labor as
those of Ireland, Dublin in particular. Many had come
to the cities from farms, which could no longer sustain
them. Living in slums and surrounded by disease and
corruption, they provided a pool of cheap labor for
Irish entrepreneurs.

In 1908 James Larkin (1876–1947), "the messiah of
Dublin's poor," organized the Irish Transport and
General Workers' Union, comprised of skilled and
unskilled laborers, to battle against the "dark satanic
mills" of capitalism. Larkin's weapon was the strike.
By 1913 his influence was so strong that Dublin's employers, fearing for their labor supply, formed the
Federated Employers of Dublin to break union activity. The result of union clashing with federation was
one of the most violent strike-lockouts in the history of
organized labor. It began with "Bloody Sunday," 13
August 1913, when the police charged a crowd gathered at a Larkin rally. Violence escalated in the weeks
that followed. In October the Irish Citizen Army, a
paramilitary arm of Larkin's union, was organized to
protect workers from police assault. All of Dublin was
in turmoil. As more and more workers joined the strike,
more and more employers joined the lockout.

Strike and lockout produced a chain reaction that

lasted until February 1914. But the employers—with the help of Dublin Castle, the seat of administrative government in Ireland—broke the strike. The workers gained very little practically, but they now had a sense of themselves as a potent force. Larkin himself, imprisoned briefly for sedition, went to the United States to raise funds for his union but was convicted there of anarchy and spent three years in Sing Sing.

Meanwhile, the nationalistic impulse was again gaining momentum among Irish politicians in London, who were slowly but steadfastly working toward home rule. In 1893, Gladstone's second home-rule bill for Ireland had met defeat. But in the early years of the twentieth century, a constitutional crisis in the English Parliament provided the Irish with their next move. The Liberal Party, constantly balked in their legislative proposals by the House of Lords, introduced a bill designed to limit the legislative powers of the upper house. Aware that the Liberals were dependent for a majority on Irish votes, the Irish members of the Parliament promised their support in return for a promise of home rule.

In 1911 the Liberal bill was passed, and in 1912 a new home-rule bill was introduced. It was never to reach a vote: intense opposition from Protestant Unionists of the northern Ulster province (that is, those who wanted Ireland to remain within the United Kingdom) kept the issue on the floor for two years. And in 1914 England entered into war with Germany, which was to absorb her attention for the next four years.

In Ireland, however, nationalistic sentiment had regained the revolutionary fervor of the days before the fall of Parnell. The Irish Citizen Army reorganized after the 1913 strike-lockout with a new objective. The group always remained committed to bringing about better working and living conditions for its working-class members; but now its leaders saw independence from England as the first step in achieving their socialistic goals. In 1913, another paramilitary organization, the nationalist Irish Volunteers, had been formed. Its membership included many Dublin employers, some politicians, and such upper-class figures as the social reformer Sir Roger Casement (1864–1916). The poet Padraic Pearse and Eamon de Valera (1882–1975) also belonged to the Irish Volunteers. (De Valera would become very important in Ireland's future as head of state.) There was a third active nationalist organization, the long-established secret Irish Republican Brotherhood, whose roots were in the nineteenth-century Fenian movement.

For a time, both the Irish Volunteers and the Irish Republican Army refused to identify the nationalistic cause with the special problems of labor. The Irish Citizen Army, for its part, was unwilling to embrace the "capitalist" Irish Volunteers. But James Connolly (1870–1916), a zealous socialist and high-ranking member of the Irish Citizen Army, was prepared to make compromises. Through his efforts an uneasy alliance among the three organizations was brought about.

They all did agree on one thing: England must be made to recognize Ireland's fervor for independence. Together they staged an uprising that was suicidal for its participants but the turning point in Irish history. The Easter Rebellion (or Easter Rising) began on 24 April 1916. Arms expected from Germany had not arrived; dissent within the Irish volunteers produced confusing commands and countermands; little support came from the people. Ill-prepared but determined, Ireland's champions, perhaps 1500 in all, marched out to take the English garrison in Dublin.

The English were unprepared. In the first hours of the rebellion, the rebels had the upper hand, occupying certain key buildings in the center of Dublin. At the General Post Office, they hoisted the flag of a republic, and Padraic Pearse read a proclamation of independence. It called upon all Irishmen to rise against English tyranny "in the name of God and of the dead generations." The people, however, remained confused and unmoved by Pearse's plea. The English military soon recovered from the shock of the surprise attack, gathered their forces, and retaliated by shelling the city's center with artillery.

Chaos reigned for a week before the rebellion was quashed. In the end, hundreds were dead and thousands wounded; the heart of the city was left burning and in ruins; the streets and stores were looted by the people. The patriotic zest and idealism of a few had led to the slaughter of many, rebels and innocent bystanders alike, but the rebels had achieved what they wanted—a violent demonstration of their hatred of the English.

Drumhead courts-martial followed, and the English methodically executed fifteen of the revolutionary leaders. The dispassion with which the executions were carried out created passionate revulsion among a populace hitherto indifferent. Ireland was given time to linger on the horror of the ruthless firing squads. It was difficult to forget a scene such as that of James Connolly being shot in a wheelchair. Cries of indignation came even from England, and Ireland's moderates were at last convinced of the need for Irish independence.

Public pressure halted the executions. The remaining leaders, among them Eamon de Valera, were released in a general amnesty Christmas Day 1916.

One result of the Easter Rebellion was to renew and strengthen an organization that had first emerged during the early years of the cultural revival, Sinn Féin ("we ourselves"). Its leader, Arthur Griffith (1872–

1922), had originally conceived the Sinn Féin ideal of an independent Irish economy as a complement to the cultural efforts of the Gaelic League. Although Sinn Féin began as a group of moderate home-rule advocates, many of its members had belonged to the Irish Volunteers and took part in the Easter Rebellion. By 1917, Sinn Féin had developed into a unified political party, committed to the establishment of an Irish Republic.

In the general election of 1918, Sinn Féin swept to victory, winning an overwhelming majority of the Irish seats in Parliament. They refused to take their seats. On 21 January 1919, they met in Dublin and constituted themselves an independent parliament of Ireland, the first Dáil Éireann. Eamon de Valera was elected president. The Dáil Éireann speedily set about duplicating the government machinery administered from Dublin Castle, the effect of which was to displace the established English systems, such as the justice courts.

Parliament immediately outlawed the new rebel government, but the rebels continued to build and administer their own government, covertly. At the same time, they turned to the use of underground tactics against the Royal Irish Constabulary, the policing arm of Dublin Castle. Members of the Constabulary were murdered first at long intervals and then more and more frequently. It was probably this form of terrorism that strengthened England's resolve to destroy the Dáil Éireann and regain its control of government in Ireland.

English troops were assembled and sent to the island. Most infamous among them were the Black and Tans—so-called after their half-police, half-army uniforms—whose members were recruited from the toughest ex-servicemen of World War I. The Black and Tans soon became notorious for their barbarous night raids throughout the countryside, killing or wounding many unarmed citizens. In order to combat them, members of the paramilitary groups dispersed after the Easter Rebellion formed into a new army, the Irish Republican Army, which operated in small units and employed guerrilla tactics.

The war was on. Presumably the Dáil Éireann had not been constituted with a policy of violence, but they soon issued a manifesto authorizing the slaying of "the officials and agents of the foreign invader" and the murder of "all spies, informers, and all Irishmen who act as agents for the foreigners in the warfare against us."

The particular brutality of the Anglo-Irish War (1919–21)—often euphemistically called The Troubles in Ireland—profoundly shocked the people of England. Parliament was finally persuaded to enter into negotiations with the Dáil Éireann, and, weary of violence, both sides met in England in July 1921. Delegates from the Dáil Éireann included Michael Collins (1890–1922), who had almost single-handedly planned the guerrilla tactics of the Irish Republican Army. Winston Churchill (1874–1965) and Prime Minister David Lloyd George (1863–1945) were among those who represented Parliament.

In the midst of the Anglo-Irish War, Parliament had already passed an act (1920) that granted limited self-government to a partitioned Ireland. The northern section, comprised of the six northern counties of Ulster province, and the southern section, comprised of the twenty-six remaining counties, were each to form their own parliament, but both legislatures were to remain subordinate to the English Parliament.

At the time of its passage, the home-rule and partitioning act had only intensified hostilities in the twenty-six southern counties, who demanded not merely home rule but independence. Now negotiations between

England and the Dáil Éireann resulted in a treaty that aggravated the problems even more. The six counties officially became Northern Ireland, remaining of their own volition a part of the United Kingdom. The twenty-six counties of southern Ireland became the Irish Free State; its status was that of a dominion within the English Commonwealth of Nations. The treaty was signed in December 1921 despite the adamant objections of de Valera and many other members of the Dáil Éireann and the Sinn Féin Party. They found the limited form of independence granted by England insufficient and intolerable. Moreover, they were bitterly opposed to the partition of Ireland.

Suddenly, the seeming solidarity of the ardent nationalists was demolished. On one side were the Republicans, who refused to accept the terms of the treaty and demanded an Irish Republic comprised of *all* of Ireland. On the other side were the Free Staters, who supported the treaty—although they accepted partition as only a temporary proviso. So irreconcilable were their differences that soon Irishmen were fighting Irishmen. From 1922 to 1923, Ireland was ravaged by civil war as the Irish Republican Army battled with the Free State soldiers. Men who only a year before were comrades in arms against the Black and Tans now trained their guns on one another.

Supplied with English arms, the Free State forces proved the stronger. Realizing the Republicans' cause was hopeless, de Valera and the Irish Republican Army ordered a cease-fire, "for the moment" conceding victory to "those who have destroyed the Republic."

At first the Republicans refused to run for seats in the Free State Parliament. By 1925, however, de Valera accepted the constitutional course as the only means to an independent republic—a decision that caused him to break away from Sinn Féin and form his own political party, Fianna Fail. By 1932 his party was in power and remained in power for sixteen years.

During an era of calm seldom known in Irish history, the government slowly consolidated its forces. In 1937, when de Valera became prime minister, the Irish Free State drew up a new constitution and, without incident, established itself a sovereign nation—renamed Eire—within the Commonwealth of Nations. In 1949, under John Costello's (b. 1891) ministry, Eire broke all ties with England and became the fully independent Republic of Ireland.

Thus the ideal of the champions of Ireland throughout the centuries was at last realized for most Irishmen. But for others it was not, for the problem of a divided Ireland remains to haunt the still troubled island.

In the seventeenth century, when Ulster province was "planted" with Scottish Presbyterians, Northern Ireland had come under the domination of Protestants, who today make up about two-thirds of the population there. They had opposed home-rule bills for Ireland both because of Northern Ireland's economy, which was more closely tied to England than that of its neighbor to the south, and also because they feared domination by the Catholic majority of southern Ireland. They had accepted home rule in 1920 (allowing them self-government in domestic matters only) because the measure also brought with it formal separation from southern Ireland.

This quasi-independence, however, had no benefit for the Catholic minority in Northern Ireland, who continue to be subject to discrimination in employment and housing. For many years voting laws provided for plural votes in direct proportion to the amount of property owned; thus all the poor people—most of them Catholics—were second-class citizens.

Although the voting laws have been reformed, it was a matter of too little, too late for most Catholics.

In 1969 students and intellectuals in Northern Ireland staged civil rights demonstrations protesting discriminatory practices against Catholics. The nonsectarian demonstrations, however, soon developed into riots between Catholics and Protestants. The Irish Constabulary, the official police force in Ulster, was unable to maintain peace, and, indeed, sometimes even participated in the riots on the side of the Protestants. Thus English troops were sent into the country to halt the riots.

At the outbreak of the violence, paramilitary groups quickly formed in both Catholic and Protestant communities and thwarted every attempt by England to bring about a political compromise. The Irish Republican Army, the old Republican army that had fought in the Civil War for a united Republic of Ireland, has once again gained the popular support of many Catholics. They believe any reform meaningless as long as Northern Ireland remains a part of England. They demand union with the south. On the other hand, the Ulster Defense Association, which justifies their militancy on the grounds that Protestants must be defended against the Irish Republican Army, believe that Northern Ireland must remain within the United Kingdom.

The English troops remained, but for reasons that remain controversial, their role changed drastically. They themselves became deeply involved in the violence in a complicated series of maneuvers against the Irish Republican Army and especially its breakaway, terrorist wing, the Provisionals (Provos). Attack and counterattack soon escalated into guerrilla warfare reminiscent of the Anglo-Irish War a half century earlier. Barricades were built throughout the cities and armored trucks monopolized the streets. Catholic and

Protestant citizens alike were terrorized. Forceful entry and search became commonplace; men and women were interned on suspicion and held without trial.

Seeing no other alternative to the threatening civil war, the English government assumed responsibility and placed Northern Ireland under direct rule in 1972. All attempts since then—by both the English government and Irish moderates—to bring about a Catholic-Protestant coalition and thus return the country to a viable form of self-government have failed miserably, thwarted by extremist politicians and armed militant groups. The violence in Northern Ireland continues.

Centuries of subjection to imperialistic exploitation and the resulting intricacy of political, economic, and religious strife is a history shared by all of Ireland. But the repercussions of that history have led to two very different Irelands: for one of them, the Republic of Ireland, the bitter struggle of the years is seemingly behind it; for the other, Northern Ireland, peace appears only a dim hope for the future.

BIBLIOGRAPHY

1. Plays by O'Casey

The Shadow of a Gunman and *Juno and the Paycock*. In *Two Plays*. London: Macmillan, 1925.

The Plough and the Stars. London: Macmillan, 1926.

The Silver Tassie. London: Macmillan, 1928.

Within the Gates. London: Macmillan, 1933.

The End of the Beginning and *A Pound on Demand*. In *Windfalls*. London: Macmillan, 1934.

The Star Turns Red. London: Macmillan, 1940.

Purple Dust. London: Macmillan, 1940. (Rev. ed. New York: Dramatists Play Service, 1957.)

Red Roses for Me. London: Macmillan, 1942. (Rev. ed. New York: Dramatists Play Service, 1956.)

Oak Leaves and Lavender. London: Macmillan, 1946.

Cock-a-doodle Dandy. London: Macmillan, 1949.

Hall of Healing. In *Collected Plays*, vol. 3. London: Macmillan, 1951.

Bedtime Story and *Time to Go*. In *Collected Plays*, vol. 4. London: Macmillan, 1951.

The Bishop's Bonfire. London: Macmillan, 1955.

The Drums of Father Ned. London: Macmillan, 1960.

Behind the Green Curtains, Figuro in the Night, and *The Moon Shines on Kylenamoe*. London: Macmillan, 1961.

Kathleen Listens In and *Nannie's Night Out*. In *Feath-*

ers from the Green Crow. Columbia: University of Missouri Press, 1962.

COLLECTED EDITIONS

Collected Plays. 4 vols. London: Macmillan, 1949, 1951. The following plays are included: vol. 1, *Juno and the Paycock, The Shadow of a Gunman, The Plough and the Stars, The End of the Beginning,* and *A Pound on Demand;* vol. 2, *The Silver Tassie, Within the Gates,* and *The Star Turns Red;* vol. 3, *Purple Dust, Red Roses for Me,* and *Hall of Healing;* vol. 4, *Oak Leaves and Lavender, Cock-a-doodle Dandy, Bedtime Story,* and *Time to Go.*

2. Nondramatic Works by O'Casey

AUTOBIOGRAPHIES

I Knock at the Door. London: Macmillan, 1939.
Pictures in the Hallway. London: Macmillan, 1942.
Drums under the Windows. London: Macmillan, 1945.
Inishfallen, Fare Thee Well. London: Macmillan, 1949.
Rose and Crown. London: Macmillan, 1952.
Sunset and Evening Star. London: Macmillan, 1954.

The six volumes were reprinted under the title *Mirror in My House.* 2 vols. New York: Macmillan, 1956; and under the title *Autobiographies.* 2 vols. London: Macmillan, 1963.

POETRY AND PROSE

Songs of the Wren. Dublin: Fergus O'Connor, 1918.
More Wren Songs. Dublin: Fergus O'Connor, 1918.
The Story of Thomas Ashe. Dublin: Fergus O'Connor, 1918.
The Sacrifice of Thomas Ashe. Dublin: Fergus O'Connor, 1918.
The Story of the Irish Citizen Army. Dublin: Maunsel, 1919.
Windfalls. London: Macmillan, 1934.

The Flying Wasp. London: Macmillan, 1937.

The Green Crow. New York: Braziller, 1956.

Feathers from the Green Crow: Sean O'Casey, 1905–1925. Edited by Robert Hogan. Columbia: University of Missouri Press, 1962.

Under a Colored Cap. London: Macmillan, 1963.

Blasts and Benedictions: Articles and Stories by Sean O'Casey. Selected and introduced by Ronald Ayling. London: Macmillan, 1967.

3. Works about O'Casey

Allen, J. *Masters of British Drama.* Chapt. 2. New York: Dennis Dobson, 1957.

Armstrong, W. A. *Sean O'Casey.* London: Longmans, Green, 1967.

Ayling, R. *Sean O'Casey: Modern Judgements.* London: Macmillan, 1969.

Benstock, B. *Sean O'Casey.* Lewisburg, Penn.: Bucknell University Press, 1970.

Blythe, E. *The Abbey Theatre.* Dublin: National Theatre Society, 1963.

Byrne, D. *The Story of Ireland's National Theatre: The Abbey Theatre, Dublin.* Dublin: Talbot Press, 1929.

Colum, P. *The Road Round Ireland.* New York: Macmillan, 1926.

Cowasjee, S. *O'Casey.* London: Oliver & Boyd, 1966.

Coxhead, E. *Lady Gregory: A Literary Portrait.* Chapt. 13. Rev. ed. London: Secker & Warburg, 1966.

Ellis-Fermor, U. *The Irish Dramatic Movement.* 2d ed., rev. London: Methuen, 1954.

Fallon, G. *Sean O'Casey: The Man I Knew.* London: Routledge & Kegan Paul, 1965.

Fay, G. *The Abbey Theatre: Cradle of Genius.* London: Hollis & Carter, 1958.

Findlater, R. *The Unholy Trade.* London: Gollancz, 1952.

Fraser, G. S. *The Modern Writer and his World.* Rev. ed. London: André Deutsch, 1964.

Gassner, J. *The Theatre in Our Times: A Survey of the*

Men, Materials, and Movements in the Modern Theatre. New York: Crown, 1954.

Gregory, A. *Lady Gregory's Journals: 1916–1930.* Edited by L. Robinson. London: Putnam, 1946.

————. "The Lady Gregory Letters to Sean O'Casey." Edited by A. C. Edwards. In *Modern Drama,* 8, no. 1 (1965).

Griffin, G. *The Wild Geese: Pen Portraits of Famous Irish Exiles.* London: Jarrolds, 1938.

Gwynn, S. *Irish Literature and Drama in the English Language.* London: Nelson, 1936.

Henn, T. R. *The Harvest of Tragedy.* London: Methuen, 1956.

Hodson, J. L. *No Phantoms Here.* London: Faber, 1932.

Hogan, R. *The Experiments of Sean O'Casey.* New York: St. Martin's Press, 1960.

————. *After the Irish Renaissance: A Critical History of the Irish Drama since "The Plough and the Stars."* Minneapolis: University of Minnesota, 1967.

Kavanagh, P. *The Story of the Abbey Theatre.* New York: Devin-Adair, 1950.

Knight, G. W. *The Golden Labyrinth: A Study of British Drama.* New York: Norton, 1962.

Koslow, J. *Sean O'Casey: The Man and His Plays.* Rev. ed. New York: Citadel Press, 1966.

Krause, D., ed. *The Letters of Sean O'Casey.* Vol. 1 (1910–41). New York: Macmillan, 1975.

————. *Sean O'Casey: The Man and His Work.* New York: Macmillan, 1960.

Krutch, J. W. *"Modernism" in Modern Drama: A Definition and an Estimate.* Chapt. 5. New York: Cornell University Press, 1953.

Lewis, A. *The Contemporary Theatre: The Significant Playwrights of Our Time.* Chapt. 9. New York: Crown, 1962.

McCann, S., ed. *The World of Sean O'Casey.* London: Four Square Books, 1966.

MacDiarmid, H. *The Company I've Kept: Essays in Autobiography.* London: Hutchinson, 1966.

Malone, A. E. *The Irish Drama, 1896–1928.* London: Constable, 1929. Republished, New York: Benjamin Blom, Inc., 1965.

Malone, M. *The Plays of Sean O'Casey.* Carbondale and Edwardsville: Southern Illinois University Press, 1969.

Margulies, M. *The Early Life of Sean O'Casey.* Chester Springs: University of Pennsylvania, 1970.

Mikhail, E. H. *Sean O'Casey: A Bibliography of Criticism.* Seattle: University of Washington Press, 1972.

Mikhail, E. H., and O'Riordan, J., eds. *The Sting and the Twinkle: Conversations with Sean O'Casey.* New York: Harper & Row, 1974.

O'Casey, E. *Sean.* New York: Coward, McCann & Geoghegan, 1972.

Robinson, L. *Curtain Up: An Autobiography.* London: Michael Joseph, 1942.

———. *Ireland's Abbey Theatre: A History, 1899–1951.* Port Washington, N.Y.: Kennikat Press, 1951.

———, ed. *The Irish Theatre: Lectures Delivered during the Abbey Theatre Festival Held in Dublin in August 1938.* London: Macmillan, 1939.

Ryan, D. *Remembering Sion: A Chronicle of Storm and Quiet.* London: Arthur Barker, 1934.

Skelton, R., and Clark, D. R., eds. *Irish Renaissance: A Gathering of Essays, Memoirs, and Letters from the Massachusetts Review.* Dublin: Dolmen Press, 1965.

Thompson, W. I. *The Imagination of an Insurrection: Dublin, Easter 1916.* Chapt. 7. London: Oxford University Press, 1967.

Trewin, J. C. *Dramatists of Today.* London: Staples Press, 1953.

See also *The Sean O'Casey Review,* edited by Robert G. Lowery.

INDEX